S. Hrg. 113–552

COMBATING VIOLENCE AND DISCRIMINATION AGAINST WOMEN: A GLOBAL CALL TO ACTION

HEARING

BEFORE THE

SUBCOMMITTEE ON INTERNATIONAL OPERATIONS AND ORGANIZATIONS, HUMAN RIGHTS, DEMOCRACY, AND GLOBAL WOMEN'S ISSUES

OF THE

COMMITTEE ON FOREIGN RELATIONS UNITED STATES SENATE

ONE HUNDRED THIRTEENTH CONGRESS

SECOND SESSION

JUNE 24, 2014

Printed for the use of the Committee on Foreign Relations

Available via the World Wide Web: http://www.gpo.gov/fdsys/

U.S. GOVERNMENT PUBLISHING OFFICE

93–138 PDF　　　　　WASHINGTON : 2015

For sale by the Superintendent of Documents, U.S. Government Publishing Office
Internet: bookstore.gpo.gov　Phone: toll free (866) 512–1800; DC area (202) 512–1800
Fax: (202) 512–2104　Mail: Stop IDCC, Washington, DC 20402–0001

CONTENTS

COMBATING VIOLENCE AND DISCRIMINATION AGAINST WOMEN: A GLOBAL CALL TO ACTION

TUESDAY, JUNE 24, 2014

U.S. SENATE, SUBCOMMITTEE ON INTERNATIONAL OPERATIONS AND ORGANIZATIONS, HUMAN RIGHTS, DEMOCRACY, AND GLOBAL WOMEN'S ISSUES, COMMITTEE ON FOREIGN RELATIONS,

Washington, DC.

The subcommittee met, pursuant to notice, at 9:50 a.m., in room SD–419, Dirksen Senate Office Building, Hon. Barbara Boxer, chairman of the subcommittee, presiding.

Present: Senators Boxer, Menendez, Durbin, Markey, Paul, and Risch.

OPENING STATEMENT OF HON. BARBARA BOXER, U.S. SENATOR FROM CALIFORNIA

Senator BOXER. Good morning, everybody.

Our women Senate colleagues will be coming in as they can. We have a whole series of votes starting at 11 o'clock. So we are going to do our best to move along, combining the last two panels, et cetera. But I certainly want to welcome everyone to today's hearing.

I am going to ask Senators to try to do our opening in about 4 minutes, if we can. Okay? Four minutes for Senators. Then we hope our panels will be as brief as they can.

Welcome, Senator Baldwin.

I want to welcome everybody to today's hearing. I am so pleased that my ranking member is here and I am so excited that the chairman of the full committee is here. It means a lot to me, but more importantly, it means a lot to the women of the world. And of course, my colleagues, my female Senate colleagues—their voices are so powerful.

We are here today because we all share the same goal: to eliminate violence and discrimination against women everywhere.

Just last month, two young Indian girls were found dead hanging from a tree after they had been raped and strangled.

In Pakistan, a 25-year-old pregnant woman was stoned to death by her family for marrying against their wishes.

In April, more than 200 Nigerian school girls were abducted from their boarding school by the terrorist group, Boko Haram.

Tragically even in the year 2014, the state of women around the world remains precarious. Every day women and girls endure hor-

(1)

rific acts of violence in their homes and communities. Women are raped, beaten, disfigured by acid, forcibly married, trafficked and sold as slaves. They are denied basic rights—such as the opportunity to get an education, to see a doctor, try to make a living outside the home—simply because of their gender.

But we have an opportunity to take action to help end the scourge of violence and discrimination against women, and that is why I introduced the International Violence Against Women Act, IVAWA, with Senators Menendez, Collins, Kirk, and Shaheen. And we have so many supporters on that bill now. And it is why I have long supported U.S. ratification of CEDAW, the Convention on the Elimination of All Forms of Discrimination Against Women.

I hope this hearing builds momentum for action in the Senate on both IVAWA and CEDAW because we have to do more than make our speeches and call for an end to violence. We have to act.

I am so proud that we will hear from not only my colleagues on the committee but some of the great women of the Senate, and I thank them for joining us today.

I am going to turn first, if it okay with Senator Menendez, to my ranking member and then to Senator Menendez.

OPENING STATEMENT OF HON. RAND PAUL, U.S. SENATOR FROM KENTUCKY

Senator PAUL. Thank you.

The great Pakistani poet, Parveen Shakir, wrote: "They insist upon evaluating the firefly in the daylight. The children of our age have grown clever."

Malala Yousafzai never met the great Urdu poet, Parveen Shakir, as their lives missed each other by several years. Shakir's life was cut short by an auto accident in 1994. But Malala's courage, vibrancy, and wit would have her smile. It would have made her proud that a young woman was standing up so strongly.

Unfortunately now, because of the actions of extremists in the Pakistani Taliban, young women must fight for the right to go to school. Malala in her young life insisted on exposing the firefly to daylight. Her crime, as seen by the Taliban, is to believe in enlightenment, to believe that out of the darkness, tolerance can glow and overcome and overpower ignorance.

Shakir would have been pleased by Malala's actions. You see, Shakir was highly educated in a pre-Taliban Pakistan with two masters degrees and a Ph.D. She taught and published poetry to widespread acclaim.

Malala knew if the Taliban won, there would never be another Parveen Shakir to come out of Pakistan. There would never be another Benazir Bhutto. That is why she fought.

Asia Bibi is a Pakistani Christian who sits on death row for blasphemy. She says it all began when she drew water from a Muslim well. As she was filling her bowl with water, the crowd formed chanting, "Death. Death to the Christian." She pleaded for her life. She was pelted with stones, punched in the face, and dragged through the streets. The local imam finally intervened only to say, "If you don't want to die, convert to Islam."

The crowd descended on her again, pelting her with sticks and stones. Finally, the police stopped the attack and she was grateful, only to be arrested by the police for blasphemy. She has been sitting for 5 years on death row in Pakistan.

Meanwhile, the U.S. taxpayer has forked over billions of dollars to the Pakistani Government, which officially condones the persecution of Christians. Many countries that receive U.S. foreign aid have laws that officially discriminate against Christians and women. Persecution of women is wrong. Persecution of Christians is wrong. Persecution of women or Christians in the name of any religion is wrong, and our aid money should have conditions upon it. We should not give one dime of aid to countries that persecute women or Christians.

Some say our aid projects our power. These same people, though, resist any conditions on our aid. Time after time, I have attempted to attach restrictions to aid to Egypt, to Pakistan, to the Palestinian Authority, and yet the majority in Congress and in the Senate has resisted every attempt to attach conditions. We should not send aid to countries who have official policies that discriminate against women and religious liberty.

We are being taxed to send money to countries that are not only intolerant of Christians but openly hostile. Christians are imprisoned and threatened with death for their beliefs. Our job as the powerful is to use our might to speak to those who cannot. Whether that is the bully pulpit of our foreign aid, our State Department, our immigration policy, or our trade policy, we should not be giving money without restrictions to people who violate basic human rights.

I am glad to be a part of this, and I think this is a good step forward. Thank you, Chair.

Senator BOXER. Thank you, Senator.

Mr. Chairman Menendez.

OPENING STATEMENT OF HON. ROBERT MENENDEZ, U.S. SENATOR FROM NEW JERSEY

Senator MENENDEZ. Let me thank my friend and colleague, Senator Boxer, for chairing an important hearing with so many distinguished women.

I was honored to cosponsor with Senator Boxer the International Violence Against Women Act that provides critically needed tools that the United States could use to address the persistent, horrific violence against women around the world.

But we must also continue to build support for the ratification of the Convention on the Elimination of All Forms of Discrimination Against Women. CEDAW has been pending before the Senate since November 1980.

So today we are shining a light on the importance of preventing and responding to gender-based violence, and it is clear from just reading the morning paper, stories on South Sudan, Iraq, Nigeria, Syria, Egypt, India, and Pakistan, that gender-based violence is a global epidemic. This is a fight that demands action from every single one of us, women and men alike. When hundreds of girls are kidnapped by Boko Haram in Nigeria or women in Afghanistan are raped, burned with the acid, or subjected to brutal violence, when these horrific acts are committed, it strains the imagination and stains the conscience of the global community.

So everyone in this room, I believe, thanks you, Senator Boxer, for being there for every woman in America and around the world who needs a champion. And there are many.

In too many places, women are producing 70 percent of the food, but earning only 10 percent of the income and own only 1 percent of the land. In too many places, women are banned from participating in national governments, village councils, and peace negotiations. In too many places, girls are prevented from attending school, and now a majority of the world's illiterate people are women. In too many places women and girls are attacked as a deliberate and coordinated strategy of armed conflict, and rape is used as a weapon of war.

And in spite of all of that horrific news, there is also some good news. In Uganda, a robust women's movement began a tireless campaign to ensure that women were protected in the tenure, ownership, and administration of land.

In Afghanistan, life expectancy for women has risen in just 10 years from 44 years of age to 62. Ten years ago almost no girls went to school. Today 3 million are in school and make up 40 percent of all primary school enrollments. Nearly 120,000 Afghan girls have graduated from high school, 15,000 are enrolled in universities, and nearly 500 women are on university faculties.

So let me close by saying we know that when women are free of gender-based violence and allowed to be educated and safe, we know that they will make an extraordinary difference. The world needs educated women to take leadership roles, and in my view, the world needs more leaders like Senator Boxer and the panelists who are here today. And as the chairman of the Senate Foreign Relations Committee, Senator Boxer, I look forward to working with you to make both initiatives a reality.

Senator BOXER. Well, I want to thank you, Mr. Chairman, for your commitment and the same with my ranking member.

I want to say I am looking at an iconic picture here. These incredible women from all over the country—and it makes me very happy that you are here.

I have the order of arrival. I think some of you had to leave by 10:15. I think you will be okay because it is just a couple minutes each to tell a quick story. So we will start in order of arrival.

Senator Hirono.

STATEMENT OF HON. MAZIE K. HIRONO, U.S. SENATOR FROM HAWAII

Senator HIRONO. Thank you. Thank you, Chair Boxer and Ranking Member Paul, Senator Menendez, for inviting me to speak today on such an important matter.

You will be hearing incredible stories from my colleagues about discrimination against women all across our world. This violence and discrimination is rooted in sexism and disrespect toward women. And I want to share a recent example that demonstrates how high this disrespect goes.

The incident involved a Japanese female representative to the Tokyo Metropolitan Assembly, which is akin to a State government assembly in the United States. This representative, Ms. Iaku Shiamura, spoke out on the importance of supporting women who need assistance while pregnant or raising children. While she was speaking, her male counterparts in an opposing party shouted at her with comments such as, hey, idiot, hurry up and get married. Can't you have babies? Although she continued to speak, she fought back tears.

Here is a female parliamentarian who cannot even express on the assembly floor her thoughts about empowering women. Blatant disrespect and discrimination of women in the form of taunts and pigeonholing based on sex role stereotyping provides a breeding ground for more direct violence against women in the United States and around the world.

Japan, like many other countries, has a long history as a male-dominated society. This type of environment, of course, is not limited to Japan. We see echoes of it here in the United States as well. And so, yes, the United States has work to do to end discrimination and violence against women. In fact, no country is perfect in this sense. But I say that we, as women and as legislators, must continue to lead by example.

My call to action is to urge that we continue supporting all young women in pursuing all of their interests, including politics. After all, as the Civil Rights Act, Title IX—by the way, we celebrated the 42nd anniversary of the passage of Title IX yesterday—and the Violence Against Women Act showed us, changes to law made at the de jure or political level can affect the de facto discrimination women around the world face.

Thank you very much.

Senator BOXER. Senator, thank you, and I know your personal story runs deep inside you. And this is an important issue to you, and I thank you.

We will turn to Senator Klobuchar.

STATEMENT OF HON. AMY KLOBUCHAR, U.S. SENATOR FROM MINNESOTA

Senator KLOBUCHAR. Thank you very much, Chairman Boxer. Thank you to the members for holding this hearing.

I want to focus my remarks on sex trafficking. This horrific crime has emerged as the third-largest criminal enterprise in the world, behind only trafficking of guns and trafficking of drugs. The average age of girls who become victims is 13, not old enough to drive a car, not old enough to go to a high school prom.

I would like to share with you a brief story about a girl named Paloma, who Senator Heitkamp and I met in Mexico when we went down there with Cindy McCain on a trip that focused on sex trafficking a few months ago. There were girls at this shelter at Covenant House in Mexico City that were as young as age 11. Paloma was new to the house. The other girls were more adjusted. The other girls were much, I would say, friendlier and smiling, knowing that they had had horrible things happen to them. But Paloma was new to the house. And when she introduced herself, she introduced herself in English and then she just started to cry and those tears just kept coming, rolling down her cheeks.

We knew that she had suffered unspeakable abuse. We knew she was in some place that was safe. But what we did not know was what had happened to her, and I think in that way, the fact that we did not know made it all the worse. And I remember thinking, as I watched her, of meeting a refugee once who had told me that he had been through things that were so awful that it would make stones cry. That is how we felt when we met with those girls.

We have a major problem in this world. You see it in Nigeria, news today that even more children were abducted. You see it all over the world.

But what I think is important to note is that we also see it in our own country and that the major source for girls, that are sex trafficked in our own country, is our own country. And one of the things we realized, as we met with the Mexican Attorney General and the head of the Federal Police, is that we were able to say we have our own problem in this country. We want to work with you. We want to get ideas from you. We want to partner together on these prosecutions. But we have to fix things in our own country.

Senator Cornyn and I are leading a bill that has widespread bipartisan support called the Stop Exploitation Through Trafficking Act. A similar version just passed the House last month based on our bill, and we just urge this committee, in addition to the work that you will be doing, I am sure, on foreign aid and other things, to help with this problem around the world and elevate this barbaric crime as we approach foreign policy. I also ask for your support as we move forward with these sex trafficking bills that will help prosecution in our own country.

Thank you very much.

Senator BOXER. Thank you so much.

Senator Markey, would you move a little closer to us because you are too far away. [Laughter.]

No. Seriously.

Next, we will hear from Senator Stabenow.

STATEMENT OF HON. DEBBIE STABENOW, U.S. SENATOR FROM MICHIGAN

Senator STABENOW. Thank you very much, Madam Chair, for your incredible leadership and passion on this, and to our chairman of the committee who is doing such an incredible job, Ranking Member Paul, and to all of the committee.

I want to talk for a moment about what is happening in the Democratic Republic of Congo. There is a small camp of refugees right next to a national park. To get food and firewood, women in the camp are forced to go into the forest. But that forest is filled with predators, sexual predators and armed groups, who prey on these vulnerable women. On an average day, 10 women who travel into the forest are raped. Now, think about that. On an average day, 10 women going into the forest are raped. These women have no choice. If they want to cook food, if they want to stay warm at night, they need to go into the forest. And they know when they do that they are at very high risk of being attacked.

In this camp, there is a woman we call Colette. It is her job to provide counseling and support to the women who are victims of violence. She listens 10 times a day as these women recount their traumatic experiences. She guides them to emergency services that come at no cost, and she helps them to overcome the stigma and discrimination these survivors face not only from society but sometimes from their own husbands. Ten times a day Colette hears the firsthand story of a woman who is a victim of sexual violence.

Colette can relate to these women because she is a survivor herself. She was raped and she vividly remembers the fear not just of the attack but of her husband as well.

We can help these women, Madam Chair, as you know so well. International groups can provide money for firewood and fuel efficient stoves, but that is not sustainable and it does not solve the real problem.

That is why I am proud to join with you as a cosponsor of the International Violence Against Women Act. We need to put the full weight of the United States of America, our diplomacy, behind this basic human right that no woman in any country should have to live every day of their lives in fear of being attacked or raped.

Thank you.

Senator BOXER. Thank you so much.

Senator Baldwin.

STATEMENT OF HON. TAMMY BALDWIN, U.S. SENATOR FROM WISCONSIN

Senator BALDWIN. Thank you, Madam Chair.

In April 2011, 24-year-old Nicola Ngwaza was murdered in South Africa. Her attackers raped, repeatedly beat, and stabbed her apparently because of her sexual orientation, before dumping her body in a drainage ditch.

Taunts and insults against LGBTI individuals in South Africa are common as are hate crimes like sexual assault and other physical attacks, particularly in rural areas. The authority's inaction leads to a greater sense of fear and insecurity for the LGBTI community.

We often hear of the egregious acts of violence perpetrated against women in South Africa. Yet, headlines often forget to mention the violence carried out against members of the lesbian, gay, bisexual, transgender, and intersex community. Violence directed at individuals perceived to be LGBTI has steadily increased. Yet, there has been a consistent failure of police authorities to address these acts of targeted violence.

April 24, 2014 marked the 3-year anniversary of the brutal death of Nicola Ngwaza. Three years after her death, no progress has been made into the investigation of her murder, and her killer or killers remain at large.

As we hear today's testimony, we must be resolved to take action so that there are no longer stories such as Nicola's. This will take great effort from the international community and the Senate can and should contribute its part by calling up and passing bills such as your own, Madam Chairwoman, International Violence Against Women Act, and Senator Markey's International Human Rights Defense Act of 2014, both of which I am proud to join as cosponsor. These bills to help advance the cause of human rights, equality, and justice around the world are vital.

Thank you.

Senator BOXER. Thank you so much.

It is my privilege to call on Senator Heitkamp.

STATEMENT OF HON. HEIDI HEITKAMP,
U.S. SENATOR FROM NORTH DAKOTA

Senator HEITKAMP. Thank you for this wonderful event. You cannot see it, Senator, but there is a lineup outside of young women waiting to hear our voices and waiting to hear your voices because they, along with you and everyone on this panel, knows that we have leadership responsibilities and leadership obligations.

The story that I want to tell is not about a victim. It is about an activist that we met in Mexico City. Her name is Nellie Montelegra, and she singlehandedly has built out a program for prosecuting violence against women, prosecuting human trafficking, prosecuting crimes against children. And she has, along with her supporters, made a huge difference for the children and the victims of Mexico.

We stand shoulder to shoulder with all of those advocates. And I know in very many corners, there are advocates all across the country, all across the world who stand with us. But they expect one thing from us. They expect leadership. And a lot of us who confront this problem at home, confront the discussion at home as we move into a period of isolationism, a lot of us get asked why should we care. And we know those countries that are most violent against their women and children, who are most impoverished are the least stable, present the greatest national security risk. And so we have to address this problem not only from a human rights standpoint but from a national security standpoint because if we stabilize the situation, if we are able to provide for women and children in every corner of the world, we will have a much more stable, much more gracious, and I think, a much better world.

And so thank you for your leadership, and thank you for the leadership of everyone at this table.

Senator BOXER. Senator, thank you so much for putting this into a larger context.

And now we will hear from Senator Murray and our cleanup batter will be Senator Warren.

And I just want to say how proud I am, Senator Murray. I know with your leadership responsibilities, as well as all your committees, you made time for this, and it says a lot to us. Thank you.

STATEMENT OF HON. PATTY MURRAY,
U.S. SENATOR FROM WASHINGTON

Senator MURRAY. Well, thank you very much, Senator Boxer and Senator Paul. It is so important that you convened this important issue. It is something very near and dear to me and to all of us, and I appreciate the opportunity to be here with so many of our female colleagues.

I joined forces with many of the fellow Senators before you to pass the Violence Against Women Act last spring, and I said then it was one of the privileges of my career to ensure that VAWA included strong protections for tribal women, the LGBT community, and immigrants, among others. And I stand by those words today. I could not be more proud of the work we have done to advocate on behalf of women wherever they live.

But there is much more to be done especially in countries where women are still fighting for basic human rights. So I am pleased to be here today to address gender-based violence and girls' education, and I want to do so by highlighting the story of Lahli, a 15-year-old girl from India. Her story was brought to my attention by the International Center for Research on Women.

She was raised as the only daughter among four children and had to fight for food, among other resources in the family. Her own well-being was placed behind that of her brothers, despite the fact that she may very well care for her own family one day. When Lahli's mom tried to enroll her daughter in school, she was met with opposition from the elders of her community. They did not believe that the family had enough to pay for both Lahli's education and her dowry.

Eventually Lahli and her mother gave up the fight, and her dowry was deemed far more important. She was married at the young age of 15 and certainly was not ready to accept the responsibilities of matrimony. Ultimately, her marriage ended any potential opportunity to better herself and her family.

That is the fate that awaits millions of other girls in India. Girls like Lahli perpetuate a cycle that is difficult to break.

But there is a solution: invest in quality basic education. Investing in girls' education will improve the welfare of millions of people worldwide and will improve health outcomes because educated women are more likely to invest in their families and communities, and they are less likely to die in pregnancy and child birth, and their children are less likely to die in infancy. It will reduce child marriage because educated girls and women are more likely to marry later in life when they have developed the strength and maturity to accept the role with pride. And it will reduce violence because educated women are less likely to be victims of sexual or gender-based violence and are less likely to tolerate it among their families.

It is timely that on Thursday the Global Partnership for Education will hold its second replenishment pledging conference in Brussels. The partnership was actually established in 2002 in order to coordinate international resources in pursuit of a lofty goal: to deliver a good quality education to all girls and boys, prioritizing the poorest and most vulnerable. The multilateral conference will hear from nonprofit partners and governments alike about the need to invest in quality basic education.

It is my hope that the international community will heed this call so that girls like Lahli and so many like her can pursue an education, escape the trappings of poverty, and fulfill her full potential.

Thank you, Madam Chair.

Senator BOXER. Senator, thank you.

In conclusion, we hear from the Honorable Elizabeth Warren.

STATEMENT OF HON. ELIZABETH WARREN,
U.S. SENATOR FROM MASSACHUSETTS

Senator WARREN. Thank you very much. Chairman Boxer, Ranking Member Paul, members of the committee, thank you for this opportunity to discuss the importance of combating violence and discrimination against women worldwide.

I want to celebrate an inspiring woman who confronted these challenges head on from the age of 13 until her untimely death from a heart attack at the age of 48 in 2011.

Sonia Pierre was one of 12 children. She was of Haitian descent, raised in a Dominican migrant worker camp. From her early teens, Sonia dedicated her efforts toward protecting the human rights of Dominicans of Haitian descent, particularly women and children who are the most vulnerable targets of discrimination. She founded the Movement of Dominican-Haitian Women to combat gender-based discrimination and anti-Haitian prejudice and to improve women's health care services and education programs. She faced continuous physical attacks, imprisonment, and threats to her life. She was first arrested at 13 years old while marching for humane labor conditions for Haitian Dominicans working on sugar cane plantations, and she faced constant danger and attacks for the rest of her life. But she kept fighting back.

Sonia's actions in the face of these threats is an inspiration to people everywhere, but particularly to thousands of my constituents in Massachusetts, which is home to the third-largest Haitian population in the United States. Nearly 3 years after her death, Sonia's legacy of promoting the human rights of women and children of Haitian ancestry lives on.

Around the world too many women and girls confront the challenges similar to those faced by Sonia. Too many women and girls are victims of gender-based violence and discrimination as weapons of intimidation, coercion, and power. The United States must be committed to protecting the rights of women and girls committed to combating violence and discrimination against women across the globe.

Congress should pass the International Violence Against Women Act, a bill that you introduced, Chairman Boxer, and that I am proud to cosponsor with many of my colleagues, in order to strengthen existing strategies for reducing gender-based violence and discrimination worldwide. Investing in women and girls means investing in a future that is more prosperous, secure, just, and peaceful for all. And it is time for Congress to carry this fight forward. The leadership should be ours.

Thank you, Madam Chairman.

Senator BOXER. Senator, thank you.

And to my colleagues, it meant so much to me and, more importantly, to the girls and women of the world that you took time to come here today. So we will allow you to get back to your busy schedules with our deepest thanks. Thank you very much.

And we are going to combine our panels into one. As they come up, I want to hear from Senator Markey and Senator Risch, if they have opening statements.

Senator RISCH. I yield back.

Senator BOXER. So then I would ask panels two and three to come forward. There are six of you, but we need you to come as quickly as you can, given the schedule we have.

The Honorable Catherine Russell, Ambassador at Large for Global Women's Issues at the State Department; Ms. Susan Markham, Senior Coordinator for Gender Equality and Women's Empowerment, U.S. Agency for International Development. And I want to say these women work on these issues night and day.

It is actually five panelists. The next three are Mr. Gary Barker, Ph.D., international director, Promundo, Washington, DC; Ms. Jacqueline O'Neill, director, Institute for Inclusive Security, Washington, DC; and Ms. Hauwa Ibrahim, senior partner, Aries Law Firm, Nigeria.

So we will ask you all to take your seats.

Senator MARKEY. Madam Chair? Senator

BOXER. Yes.

Senator MARKEY. Maybe I could be recognized for 1 minute.

Senator BOXER. Please. Yes, Senator Markey.

STATEMENT OF HON. EDWARD J. MARKEY, U.S. SENATOR FROM MASSACHUSETTS

Senator MARKEY. I thank you, Senator Boxer, for convening this critically important hearing, and I thank all of my colleagues for your thoughtful and inspiring testimony. I think that was an incredible opening to this hearing.

According to Amnesty International, violence against women and girls is one of the most pervasive human rights abuses and a global epidemic. Almost daily we read of another woman raped, another woman murdered by an abusive spouse, another group of girls trafficked. In far too many countries, nothing is done to the perpetrators of these horrific crimes.

Violence and discrimination against women and girls is not just a human rights issue or a moral issue. It is a matter of national security. It should come as no surprise that the countries where women are safe, the countries where women are equal, are the countries with the greatest stability, both economically and politically. Where women are safe, laws are enforced. Where women are safe, girls are educated. Where women and girls are safe, women are productive, able to contribute to their families and to their communities.

That is why our foreign policy must focus laser-like on ending violence and discrimination against women and girls. That is why I am a cosponsor of your legislation and why I also introduced the International Human Rights Defense Act. We need to be sure that women's rights and LGBT rights remain a focus of our foreign policy until all women and girls around the world are free and safe and equal. We need to be sure that the positions our next witnesses, Ambassador Russell and Ms. Markham, hold are made permanent in this administration and in every administration until this epidemic of violence and discrimination ends.

Thank you, Madam Chair.

Senator BOXER. Thank you.

So here is how we are going to go. I am going to introduce the first two speakers who are our government panel, and then we will take a breath. Then I will introduce our next three speakers and then when you are all done, we will ask questions to whomever we choose.

So our first witness today is the Ambassador at Large for Global Women's Issues at the State Department, Catherine Russell. Prior to assuming this post, Ambassador Russell served as Deputy Assistant to the President and Chief of Staff to Second Lady, Dr. Jill Biden. While at the White House, Ambassador Russell coordinated the development of the administration's Strategy to Prevent and Respond to Gender-based Violence Globally, which was released in 2012. She previously served as the senior adviser to the Senate Foreign Relations Committee on international women's issues.

And I want to also welcome her brilliant staffer, Ann Norris, who learned everything she needed to learn in my office. [Laughter.]

We are very proud to see you here, Ann.

I was pleased to chair Ambassador Russell's nomination hearing last July. So I am very happy to welcome her back.

And we will then hear from Ms. Susan Markham, the Senior Co-ordinator for Gender Equality and Women's Empowerment at the U.S. Agency for International Development, USAID. Ms. Markham has a long history of working on women's political empowerment, both in the United States and globally. And most recently she served as the Director of Women's Political Participation at the National Democratic Institute, NDI, where she worked to support the meaningful participation of women around the world in civic and political life.

So thank you both for your dedicated service, and we certainly look forward to your testimony. We will begin with you, the Honorable Catherine Russell.

STATEMENT OF HON. CATHERINE M. RUSSELL, AMBASSADOR AT LARGE FOR GLOBAL WOMEN'S ISSUES, U.S. DEPARTMENT OF STATE, WASHINGTON, DC

Ambassador RUSSELL. Thank you so much. Thank you, Chairman Boxer, Senator Markey, Senator Risch, for being here.

And I just have to say, Senator Boxer, I have never seen so many amazing women lined up here today. I thought that was a very powerful statement, and I really appreciate that very much.

Before I begin, I would like to thank the subcommittee under Chairman Boxer's leadership for the tremendous work you have done to profile these issues.

I would also like to recognize my counterpart, Susan Markham, at USAID, as well as the organizations who are here today who are really indispensable partners in this work.

I want to speak today about three tools that the United States has to address and respond to the continuing epidemic of gender-based violence.

Senator Boxer, I would also like to take a moment to thank you for your support of U.S. ratification of CEDAW, which would be an important additional tool to help urge countries to meaningfully address gender-based violence, as well as other issues.

The first of our tools is diplomacy. One of my highest priorities as Ambassador is to ensure that efforts to address and end gender-based violence are a key aspect of U.S. diplomatic engagement. Gender-based violence is on the agenda of every trip I take, from encouraging the Afghan Government to fully implement the Elimination of Violence Against Women law, to meeting with survivors of acid attacks in Pakistan. Like you, I am motivated by the deeply personal stories I have heard during my travel: the young Nepalese girl whose family did not value her enough to send her to school, the young Sri Lankan woman who told me of the brutal gang rape she suffered during police interrogation, or the Afghan school girl whose father wanted to sell her rather than send her to school.

This issue is a top priority for Secretary Kerry as well. Our voices joined with yours must ring loud and clear. This violence is unacceptable.

The second powerful tool we employ in this fight is our policy efforts. This past December, the Department launched three interagency committees to implement the administration's strategy that you mentioned to prevent and respond to gender-based violence globally. To help address impunity, the United States recently suspended entry into our country of perpetrators, including government officials at any level, who are responsible for war crimes, crimes against humanity, or other serious violations of human rights, including those involving rape, sexual assault, and sexual slavery. We are encouraging other governments to take similar action to send a strong message to those who engage in these crimes.

This brings me to our third and final tool: programming to match our policy priorities and our diplomatic engagement. I would like to take a moment to highlight a number of recent efforts announced by Secretary Kerry.

First, we will soon release a new funding opportunity to build on our $10 million Safe from the Start initiative which aims to protect women and girls from the very onset in humanitarian emergencies.

Secondly, we recently announced a doubling of the original commitment in the Gender-Based Violence Emergency Response and Protection Initiative to $1 million, which provides immediate financial assistance to women and girls who have experienced severe violence or are in danger of imminent harm.

And as announced at the recent global summit in London, the United States is launching a new Accountability Initiative to help us build the capacity of partner governments to bring perpetrators to justice in innovative ways such as through the use of mobile courts.

Yet, we know that a tremendous amount of work remains to be done. In particular, we need to change mindsets so that violence against women and girls can never be dismissed as cultural or inevitable. It is criminal.

The statistics regarding gender-based violence are sobering, and yet somehow when I meet with women and girls who have faced this kind of violence, I continue to feel hopeful. The young Afghan girl I mentioned earlier, whose father wanted to sell her, was part of a larger group of girls. When I asked them what they wanted to be when they grow up, their answers were no different than the ones my daughter or her friends might give, lawyer, doctor, teacher. One wanted to be President of Afghanistan.

These girls embody promise and possibility. We know that empowering women and girls and protecting them from violence will lead to stronger families, communities, and countries. I look forward to working with you to make this a reality.

Thank you very much.

[The prepared statement of Ambassador Russell follows:]

PREPARED STATEMENT OF CATHERINE M. RUSSELL

INTRODUCTION

Good morning, and thank you, Chairman Boxer, Ranking Member Paul, and distinguished members of the committee for inviting me to testify today. I am happy to be here to discuss the importance of preventing and responding to gender-based violence and to highlight U.S. and international tools and strategies to combat violence and discrimination against women and girls globally. Before I begin, I'd like to thank this subcommittee, under Chairman Boxer's leadership, for the tremendous work you have done to raise the profile of these issues and to ensure they receive the attention they deserve. I'd also like to recognize my counterpart, Susan Markham, at USAID, as well as the NGOs in the room today who are instrumental partners in this work.

Gender-based violence, which we have seen splashed across the front pages of newspapers most recently in India, Nigeria, Pakistan—as well as here in the United States—is a global epidemic. It crosses every social and economic class, ethnicity, race, religion, and education level, and transcends international borders. It takes the form of intimate partner violence, early and forced marriages, sexual violence, acid attacks, and traditional harmful practices such as female genital mutilation/cutting. And it is widespread. Worldwide, an estimated one in three women will be physically or sexually abused in her lifetime, and one in five will experience rape or attempted rape. In some places, especially in conflict zones, these statistics are even higher. This violence doesn't only affect women and girls, but it threatens entire communities, precludes economic growth, and fuels cycles of violence and conflict.

My job as Ambassador at Large for Global Women's issues is to ensure that the rights and empowerment of women and girls are integrated into all aspects of U.S. foreign policy, to reiterate that peace, security, prosperity, and economic growth cannot be achieved without the full participation of women, and to ensure that men and boys are engaged as important partners in this effort. I believe firmly that gender-based violence is inextricably related to women's status and that we must address the issue in a comprehensive manner, including through women's economic empowerment and girls' education. I want to speak today to some of the tools we have at our disposal to address and respond to gender-based violence, and to the reasons why this topic is so critically important to the work of this administration.

TOOLS

A. Diplomacy

One of my highest priorities as Ambassador is to ensure that efforts to end gender-based violence are a key aspect of U.S. diplomatic engagement. That is why I make sure that gender-based violence is on the agenda of every trip I take and nearly every meeting I hold. These efforts range from encouraging the Afghan Government to fully implement the Elimination of Violence Against Women (EVAW) law to meeting with survivors of acid attacks in Pakistan. Like you, I am motivated by the deeply personal stories I have heard during my travel—from the young Nepalese girl whose family did not value her enough to send her to school, the Sri Lankan young woman who told me of a brutal gang rape during a police interrogation, and the Afghan schoolgirl whose father wanted to sell her rather than send her to school. We cannot rest until the violence stops.

I know that this is a priority for Secretary Kerry as well. Two weeks ago, he traveled to the United Kingdom to attend the Global Summit to End Sexual Violence in Conflict, where he powerfully stated that "Gender-based violence, anywhere, is a threat to peace, security, and dignity everywhere." He also recently visited an obstetric fistula clinic at St. Joseph's hospital in the Democratic Republic of the Congo, where some of the world's worst atrocities against women and girls are committed. Just as this is a personal priority for me, it is a priority for him. Our voices, joined with yours and with those of the survivors of gender-based violence, must ring loud and clear: it is unacceptable.

B. Policy

The second powerful tool we employ in this fight is through our policy efforts. While serving as Chief of Staff to Dr. Jill Biden, I spearheaded an interagency effort to develop the "U.S. Strategy to Prevent and Respond to Gender-Based Violence Globally," which the administration released in August 2012. This past December, the Department launched three interagency committees to implement the strategy and the accompanying Executive order from President Obama. The committees are currently working to identify focus countries, ensure that U.S programming to prevent and respond to gender-based violence is based on best practices, and implement intensive monitoring and evaluation programs for our initiatives. This work also complements and builds upon the December 2012 "U.S National Action Plan on Women, Peace and Security," which aims to protect women and advance their participation in conflict, post-conflict, and relief and recovery settings. The National Action Plan also focuses specifically on addressing gender-based violence in countries characterized by war, violence, and insecurity.

To help address impunity, Secretary Kerry recently issued a "challenge" to other governments to restrict travel by those responsible for crimes against humanity, war crimes, and other serious violations of human rights, including those involving sexual violence. The United States has suspended entry into the United States of perpetrators—including government officials, at any level—of war crimes, crimes against humanity, or other serious violations of human rights, including those involving rape, sexual assault and sexual slavery. We are hoping that other governments around the world take similar action, and we encourage you to raise this issue with them in your bilateral discussions.

All of these efforts are a direct extension of the broad gender policy initiatives undertaken by the Obama administration, which has brought an unprecedented focus to bear on promoting gender equality in service of our national security and foreign policy objectives. Advancing the status of women and girls is woven into our National Security Strategy, the QDDR, our Department of State Foreign Affairs Manual, and in policy guidance recently released by Secretary Kerry directing all bureaus and embassies to continue to further integrate gender equality in all aspects of our diplomacy, including preventing and responding to sexual violence in peacetime and conflict.

C. Programming

This brings to me to my third and final tool: programming to match our policy priorities and our diplomatic engagement. We recognize that prevention and response to gender-based violence is a critical part of our work, and I'd like to take a moment to highlight a number of recent efforts announced by Secretary Kerry. These efforts build upon long-standing work being done by the Department and USAID on this issue.

First, we will soon release a new funding opportunity to build on our $10 million Safe from the Start Initiative. Safe from the Start is a joint State-USAID effort that focuses on getting the right systems in place at the very onset of a conflict or crisis. The United States has already provided support to the Office of the High Commissioner for Refugees (UNHCR) and the International Committee of the Red Cross (ICRC) to help hire specialized staff and to develop innovative methods to protect women and girls at the onset of emergencies worldwide. We know that women and girls are most at risk in these settings, and we must make every effort to ensure their safety.

Second, we recently announced a doubling of the original commitment to the Gender-Based Violence Emergency Response and Protection Initiative to $1 million. This initiative addresses the immediate security needs of survivors of severe gender-based violence, as well as individuals under credible threat of imminent attack due to their gender. Individuals can quickly receive U.S. assistance for up to 6 months, reaching a total of $5,000. These flexible funds can be used to address short-term emergency needs such as payment of legal and medical bills, relocation, security, and dependent support. This fund provides a mechanism to respond immediately to the horrible stories of violence we read about so often in the news. In addition, it also provides targeted training to implement gender-based violence laws and support activism to address cultural attitudes and norms around gender-based violence.

Third, the United States just committed an additional $2.5 million to expand our partnerships with countries undertaking Centers for Disease Control and Prevention (CDC) National Violence Against Children Surveys along with the global public-private partnership Together for Girls. Together for Girls, which the United States Government helped to launch, helps countries undertake comprehensive surveys to document the magnitude, nature, and impact of physical, emotional and sexual violence against children with a specific focus on girls. Based on this data, Together for Girls helps implement evidence-based coordinated policy and program actions to address issues identified through the surveys, including legal and policy reforms, improved services for children who have experienced violence, and prevention programs.

And finally, as announced at the Global summit in London, the United States is launching a new Accountability Initiative to help survivors of gender-based violence access the justice they deserve. This effort will help us build the capacity of partner governments to prosecute sexual violence crimes and bring perpetrators to justice through specialized judicial mechanisms in countries ravaged by war, violence, and insecurity. As you know, many countries facing serious sexual violence crimes often lack functioning judicial systems. This initiative is designed to send a strong message to would-be perpetrators that they will be held accountable for their crimes.

In addition to these recent announcements, the Department of State runs a variety of programs focused on preventing and responding to gender-based violence. For example, through our Bureau of International Narcotics and Law Enforcement Affairs, we are currently funding women's protective shelters in Afghanistan. One of our largest programs, the President's Emergency Plan for AIDS Relief (PEPFAR) specifically addresses the link between gender-based violence and HIV/AIDS. My own office has administered a series of small grants over the past few years to support civil society organizations working in their communities to address gender-based violence. I would be happy to share more information about these efforts.

Yet we know that a tremendous amount of work remains to be done. We need additional research and data on best practices to end this global scourge, and we need to know more about how best to engage men and boys, who often serve as leaders in the community. Finally, we need to change mindsets so that it is clear to everyone that violence against women and girls can never be dismissed as cultural or inevitable—it is criminal.

Gender-based violence is a collective problem that demands a collective solution—it requires not only the expertise of private, public, and nonprofit sectors, but the commitment of the global community. The United States will continue to be a vocal advocate on this issue in the multilateral space, including at the Commission on the Status of Women and the U.N. General Assembly.

The statistics regarding gender-based violence are sobering, and the challenge and needs are great. And yet, somehow when I meet with women and girls who have faced this kind of violence, I walk away feeling reenergized. The young Afghan girl I mentioned earlier in my testimony—whose father wanted to sell her—was part of a larger group of girls I spoke with. When I asked them what they wanted to be when they grew up, their answers were no different than the ones my own daughter might give: lawyer, doctor, teacher. One girl said she wanted to be President.

These girls embody promise and possibility. We know that empowering women and girls and protecting them from violence will lead to stronger families, communities, and countries. I look forward to working with you to make this a reality.

Senator BOXER. Thank you.
And we will turn to Ms. Susan Markham.

STATEMENT OF SUSAN MARKHAM, SENIOR COORDINATOR FOR GENDER EQUALITY AND WOMEN'S EMPOWERMENT, U.S. AGENCY FOR INTERNATIONAL DEVELOPMENT, WASHINGTON, DC

Ms. MARKHAM. Thank you. Good morning, Chairwoman Boxer, Senators Durbin and Risch, and other distinguished members of the subcommittee. Thank you for the opportunity to testify before you today regarding the critical issue of gender-based violence.

And, Senator Boxer, I must say we appreciate your years of work on behalf of women and girls around the world.

Under the leadership of President Obama, the United States has put gender equality and the advancement of women and girls at the forefront of U.S. foreign policy, and preventing and responding to gender-based violence is a cornerstone of the administration's commitment to advancing gender equality.

Gender-based violence cuts across ethnicity, race, sexual orientation, class, religion, educational level, and even international borders. The majority of survivors are women and girls, but men and boys are also subjected to this crime. An estimated one in three women worldwide has been beaten, coerced into sex, or otherwise abused in her lifetime with intimate partner violence as the most common form of violence experienced by women globally.

Gender-based violence can also take the form of harmful traditional practices such as female genital mutilation or cutting, so-called honor killings, bride abductions, and early enforced marriage.

For over two decades, USAID has partnered with nongovernmental, public international, and faith-based organizations, as well as host government institutions, to address the issue of gender-based violence. USAID programs focus on four strategies to combat gender-based violence.

First, we address the root causes of violence.

Next, we increase the awareness of the scope and impact of gender-based violence.

We also try to work to improve services for the survivors of violence.

And finally, we support legal frameworks to strengthen prevention efforts.

In the last 2 years, USAID has reinvigorated its work on gender equality and women's empowerment, launching a number of complementary policies and strategies to bolster our efforts, building on our expertise in development assistance to maximize the impact of agency efforts to prevent and respond to gender-based violence.

All USAID gender-based violence programs seek to reach the most vulnerable populations, including women, children, persons with disabilities, lesbian, gay, bisexual, and transgender persons, and the elderly who often face extraordinary levels of violence and abuse.

Poverty, social norms, and the imbalance of power between men and women are often drivers of gender-based violence. So in South Africa, USAID is supporting the scale-up of the Intervention with Microfinance for AIDS and Gender Equity project, called IMAGE, and findings from this work indicate that economic and social empowerment of women can contribute to reductions in intimate partner violence.

USAID recognizes that protection of vulnerable populations must be addressed in both public and private spaces. So USAID's Safe Schools pilot program worked to reduce gender-based violence in schools in Ghana and Malawi for 30,000 girls and boys. By the end of the project, teachers and students exhibited changed attitudes about gender-based violence.

The most effective approaches to providing services to survivors are often holistic. So in 2013, USAID's Victim of Torture program in the Democratic Republic of Congo reached more than 42,000 beneficiaries to provide medical treatment, psychological and social support, legal assistance, awareness raising, and economic strengthening.

Strengthening laws and policies is also critical in combating gender-based violence. In 2013, USAID provided funding to support a state-of-the-art training in the Middle East and North Africa that expanded the number and regional diversity of experts with the capacity to investigate these kinds of crimes.

Looking ahead, USAID will continue to refine tools and interventions to effectively address gender-based violence. The agency is actively involved in finding ways to adopt appropriate technology that will provide innovative, effective, and cost-effective solutions while also encouraging stronger evaluations of activities that address gender-based violence.

As mentioned by my colleague, Ambassador Russell, the Safe from the Start initiative is a joint USAID and State Department effort to build capacity of the humanitarian system to better meet the women and girls in emergency situations.

USAID will continue to address gender-based violence through partnerships with host communities, civil society organizations, universities, donor organizations, foundations, and private companies.

Chairman Boxer, thank you once again for the opportunity to speak to this vitally important issue.

[The prepared statement of Ms. Markham follows:]

PREPARED STATEMENT OF SUSAN MARKHAM

Good afternoon, Chairwoman Boxer, Ranking Member Paul, and distinguished members of the subcommittee. Thank you for the opportunity to testify before you today regarding the critical issue of gender-based violence. It is an honor to be joined by my colleague from the State Department and by others working to effect change on this issue.

Under the leadership of President Obama, the United States has put gender equality and the advancement of women and girls at the forefront of the three pillars of U.S. foreign policy—diplomacy, development, and defense. This is embodied in the President's National Security Strategy, the Presidential Policy Directive on Global Development, and the 2010 U.S. Quadrennial Diplomacy and Development Review. Women's empowerment is critical to USAID's core mission of ending extreme poverty and promoting resilient, democratic societies while advancing our security and prosperity and addressing pressing health and education challenges.

Preventing and responding to gender-based violence is a cornerstone of the administration's commitment to advancing gender equality. Such violence is often a direct result of existing inequalities and hinders the ability of individuals to fully participate in and contribute to their families and communities—economically, politically, and socially.

The United States Congress, and this committee in particular, has long championed efforts to prevent and respond to gender-based violence. As a result of these tireless efforts, Congress has been a key driver in responding to gender-based violence in the context of early and forced marriage, female genital mutilation/cutting, and region-specific violence against women, from Latin America and the Caribbean to the Middle East and North Africa. Congress has played a critical role in highlighting the bipartisan commitment of the United States to preventing and responding to gender-based violence, and has helped strengthen ongoing U.S. efforts.

STATEMENT OF THE PROBLEM AND STATISTICS

The United States has a strong interest in preventing and responding to gender-based violence around the world. Regardless of the form that gender-based violence takes, it is a human rights abuse, a public health challenge, and a barrier to civic, social, political, and economic participation. It leads to many negative consequences, including adverse physical and mental health outcomes, limited access to education, increased costs relating to medical and legal services, lost household productivity, and reduced income.

Gender-based violence cuts across ethnicity, race, sexual orientation, class, religion, education level, and international borders. The majority of survivors are women and girls, but men and boys are also subjected to this crime. An estimated one in three women worldwide has been beaten, coerced into sex, or otherwise abused in her lifetime, with intimate partner violence as the most common form of violence experienced by women globally. An appalling 38 percent of all murders of women globally were reported being committed by their partners. Gender-based violence can also take the form of harmful traditional practices, such as female genital mutilation/cutting, so-called "honor killings," bride abductions, and early and forced marriage.

An estimated 10 million girls are married every year before they reach 18. Early and forced marriage is a practice that increases a girl's risk of school dropout, maternal mortality, short birth intervals, and vulnerability to other forms of gender-based violence, among other adverse outcomes. Children are particularly vulnerable to violence, especially sexual abuse. According to the United Nations Population Fund, almost 50 percent of all sexual assaults worldwide are against girls 15 and younger. In 2002, 150 million girls and 73 million boys under the age of 18 years experienced forced sexual intercourse or other forms of sexual violence. Sexual violence is also often used as a tactic of war during conflicts. In the context of humanitarian crises and emergencies, civilian women and children are often the most vulnerable to exploitation, violence, and abuse because of their gender, age, and status in society. Women with a disability are two to three times more likely to suffer physical and sexual abuse than women with no disability. Lesbian, gay, bisexual, and transgender persons also face heightened risk. Sexual violence can also directly lead to HIV infection. Gender-based violence can foster the spread of HIV by limiting one's ability to negotiate safe sexual practices, disclose HIV status, and access services due to fear of reprisal.

Gender-based violence undermines the safety, dignity, health, and human rights of survivors as well as the public health, economic stability, and security of nations. The United Nations Secretary General's 2005 in-depth study on violence against women found that when calculated across 13 countries (Australia, Bangladesh, Canada, Chile, Finland, Jamaica, Nicaragua, Netherlands, New Zealand, Spain, Switzerland, United Kingdom, and United States) the cost amounted to USD50 billion per year.

USAID WORK ON GENDER-BASED VIOLENCE

For over two decades, USAID has partnered with nongovernmental organizations, public international organizations, faith-based organizations, and host government institutions to increase awareness of the scope and impact of gender-based violence, improve services for survivors of violence, and strengthen prevention efforts.

Over the last 2 years, USAID has reinvigorated and strengthened its work on gender equality and women's empowerment, launching a number of new complementary policies and strategies to bolster and leverage our efforts. These policies include USAID's ''Gender Equality and Female Empowerment Policy,'' which provides guidance to our staff in Washington and in the field on pursuing more effective, evidence-based investments in gender equality and female empowerment and incorporating these efforts into our core development programming. The ''U.S. National Action Plan on Women, Peace, and Security'' focuses on gender equality and women's empowerment in crisis and conflict-affected countries to promote the rights and well-being of women and girls and to foster peaceful, resilient communities that can cope with adversity and pursue development gains. The ''U.S. Strategy to Prevent and Respond to Gender-Based Violence'' established a government-wide approach that identifies, coordinates, integrates, and leverages current efforts and resources. The ''U.S. Government Action Plan on Children in Adversity'' is the first-ever whole-of-government strategic guidance on international assistance for children in adversity integrating assistance and measuring results to ensure that children ages 0–18 not only survive, but thrive. The ''USAID Vision for Action: Ending Child Marriage and Addressing the Needs of Married Adolescents'' highlights the need for development efforts to combat early and forced marriage and focus on regions, countries, and communities where interventions to prevent and respond to early and forced marriage are most needed and most likely to achieve results. The updated President's Emergency Plan for AIDS Relief (PEPFAR) gender strategy prioritizes gender-based violence prevention activities as well as the provision of post gender-based violence care, and also seeks to address the harmful norms that perpetuate such violence. And finally, the ''USAID Counter-Trafficking in Persons Policy'' reinvigorates and focuses Agency efforts to combat trafficking on concrete, measurable principles and objectives.

USAID's aspiration is simple—to use this framework to build on its global reach and expertise in development and humanitarian assistance to maximize the impact of Agency efforts to prevent and respond to gender-based violence.

USAID supports many programs that prevent and respond to gender-based violence around the world. All USAID gender-based violence programs seek to reach the most vulnerable populations—including women, children, persons with disabilities, lesbian, gay, bisexual, and transgendered persons and the elderly—who often face extraordinary levels of violence and abuse. Sadly, women and children often fare the worst in war, and gender-based violence rates often increase in complex crises around the world. Gender-based violence threatens to undermine the rights and security of women and girls—and even boys and men. It also threatens to stall or even reverse the important development gains made in many of the countries in which USAID works.

Since 2013, USAID has funded 25 humanitarian assistance programs designed to prevent and/or respond to gender-based violence in countries affected by conflict and natural disaster, including the Democratic Republic of Congo, Syria, South Sudan, and the Central African Republic.

USAID programs address the root causes of violence, improve prevention and protection services, respond to the health and economic needs of those affected by gender-based violence, and support legal frameworks that mitigate gender-based violence. Within these programs, USAID works to engage women and girls—and to engage men and boys as advocates to both prevent and respond to sexual harassment and assault.

Addressing the root causes of violence

Poverty, social norms, and the imbalance of power between men and women are often drivers of gender-based violence. In South Africa, USAID is supporting the scale-up of the Intervention with Microfinance for AIDS and Gender Equity (IMAGE) Project. The IMAGE project sought to find evidence about the scope of women's empowerment and the mechanisms underlying the significant reduction in intimate partner violence documented by the cluster-randomized trial in rural South Africa. The findings, both qualitative and quantitative, indicate that economic and social empowerment of women can contribute to reductions in intimate partner violence. The IMAGE intervention combined a microfinance program with participatory training on understanding HIV infection, gender norms, domestic violence, and sexuality. After 2 years, the risk of past-year physical or sexual violence by an intimate partner was reduced by more than half.

Improve prevention and protection services

USAID recognizes that protection of vulnerable populations must be addressed in both public and private spaces. USAID's Safe Schools Pilot Program worked to reduce school-related gender-based violence in selected schools in Ghana and Malawi and to support prevention programs and support services for 30,000 girls and boys. By the end of the project, teachers and students exhibited changed attitudes about gender-based violence. The program was scaled up and launched in the Dominican Republic, Senegal, Yemen, Tajikistan, and the Democratic Republic of Congo. In addition, USAID has formed a partnership with the Peace Corps to use the Safe Schools materials and train volunteers on how to create a safe classroom environment, integrate gender-equitable practices into teaching and classroom management, and promote primary school reading.

Gender-based violence is a long-standing problem in Haiti where the risk of violence and sexual exploitation is exacerbated by poverty, poor security, and a lack of awareness. USAID provided direct support and technical assistance to the Ministry of Women's Affairs for a campaign against rape. In addition, USAID is training Haitian health care providers at 31 facilities on how to identify and manage gender-based violence cases and provide referrals to social and legal services. Since 2012, more than 177,000 people have been surveyed and sensitized on gender-based violence, including 485 staff, over 118,000 patients, and over 58,500 community members living in high-risk areas.

Because the crisis in Syria is fundamentally a failure of protection of the civilian population, our overall humanitarian response strategy within Syria is informed by a protection analysis and includes measures to promote the protection of the population—including prevention of, and response to, gender-based violence. Our five protection priorities to address the crisis in Syria are gender and protection mainstreaming, gender-based violence prevention and response, child protection, psychosocial support, and humanitarian access. Additionally, specific activities include improving access to urgent clinical care and support, establishment of safe healing and learning spaces, basic needs provision, livelihoods opportunities and emergency shelters, and, within refugee hosting communities, efforts to prevent early marriage, human trafficking, child labor and domestic violence.

Responding to health and economic needs

Effective approaches to providing services to survivors are most often holistic in nature. This includes improving access to comprehensive sexual and reproductive health services and mental health care for survivors of sexual violence so that they can rebuild their lives on their own terms, and physically and emotionally move beyond the point in time when they were victims of assault. In 2013, USAID's Victims of Torture program in the Democratic Republic of the Congo in the geographical areas of North and South Kivu reached more than 42,000 beneficiaries to provide medical treatment, psychological and social support, legal assistance, awareness raising and economic strengthening. An impact evaluation of the mental health components of this program documented positive results for survivors participating in therapy, validating research tools that can be applied to similar programs in low-resource settings. For example, in this case we learned that women who participated in group cognitive processing therapy experienced a stronger reduction of post-traumatic stress disorder symptoms than women who received individual counseling. Having these tools helps us design tailored approaches that are effective for supporting survivors in different contexts.

Through the Gender Equity Program in Pakistan, USAID is providing social and economic rehabilitation of gender-based violence survivors by supporting 12 shelters and helplines across Pakistan. Through this model, thousands of gender-based violence survivors in Pakistan are receiving legal services, psychosocial counseling, technical and vocational skills training, and economic rehabilitation services for the first time. The successful implementation of this model has attracted government shelters to adopt a similar approach. The Gender Equity Program has also developed a strategy on combating gender-based violence which will work as a guideline for the provincial governments on addressing gender-based violence issues. The strategy has already been endorsed by three provincial governments.

Supporting legal frameworks to mitigate gender-based violence

This type of engagement with local governments to strengthen laws and policies is critical in combating gender-based violence. Even as we strengthen our support for survivors, we know that impunity for conflict-related sexual violence and other forms of gender-based violence is a major challenge for prevention. In 2013, USAID provided funding to support a state-of-the art training with Justice Rapid Response on the investigation of gender-based violence under international law. The training expanded the number and regional diversity of experts available to serve on a dedicated roster of gender-based violence experts that provides the international community with a rapidly deployable, standby capacity to investigate these crimes. The training focused on Middle East and North Africa regional experts and Arabic-speaking interpreters. We anticipate that some of these participants will serve on commissions of inquiry looking into allegations of human rights violations and abuses in the Middle East and North Africa region.

USAID in El Salvador is working with the judicial system, the Attorney General's Office, the national police, and the Salvadoran Institute for the Development of Women to ensure domestic and sexual violence survivors receiving humane, efficient, and professional treatments. The project also focuses on training police officers and judicial staff across the country to protect and respond to the needs of survivors who are often forgotten. With USAID's support, 16 Victims Assistance Centers have opened, and there will be a total of 31 centers by 2018.

LOOKING AHEAD

Looking ahead, USAID will continue to refine tools and interventions to effectively address gender-based violence. USAID is developing sector-specific toolkits that will help project design teams, project managers, and program officers integrate gender-based violence prevention and response efforts into USAID programs. USAID will continue to provide resources and training to staff to assist them with integrating gender-based violence issues into their work.

The Agency is actively involved in finding ways to adopt appropriate technology that provides innovative, effective, and cost-efficient solutions to address gender-based violence. USAID cosponsored a "Gender-Based Violence and Innovative Technologies: Opportunities, Challenges and Ethical Considerations" event to bring together select researchers and programmers from the United States and abroad who are implementing innovative technologies to address gender-based violence in a range of settings.

USAID and many other Agencies, donors and foundations have invested in programs to prevent and respond to gender-based violence; however, there have not been enough rigorous evaluations of these programs to investigate what aspects of programs addressing gender-based violence are successful and what may need adjustment. USAID will continue to encourage stronger evaluations of activities that address gender-based violence.

USAID has invested in numerous research studies focused on understanding the gaps in preventing and responding to gender-based violence. In India, USAID is supporting research on the effectiveness of conditional cash transfers on delaying marriage among girls until the age of 18. In Uganda, USAID is investing in research to evaluate the effects of innovative scalable behavior change communication programs to prevent gender-based violence, which focus on working with adolescents and community gatekeepers to promote and establish gender equitable norms, as well as engaging fathers to promote positive parenting roles and to reduce conflict between men and their wives. In Pakistan, research on the scope and scale of violence against women has resulted in more targeted, regionally specific interventions and ultimately more effective service provision for survivors. In Afghanistan, USAID recently finalized a study on engaging men in ending gender-based violence and is funding the upcoming Demographic and Health Survey, which will generate detailed data on gender-based violence trends. The Afghan Government will use the survey to develop programs to address gender-based violence issues.

In September 2013, Secretary of State John Kerry announced the Safe from the Start initiative, a joint USAID and State Department effort to build capacity of the humanitarian system for timely, quality and effective prevention and response. Agency resources are being used to support strategic investments to close knowledge and capacity gaps, enhance accountability to ensure gender-based violence prevention and response are a priority from the onset of an emergency, and build on the significant humanitarian funding State and USAID provide to prevention and response efforts each year. Safe from the Start also represents the U.S. Government's commitments to the Call to Action, a closely related, multicountry effort launched by the United Kingdom last year which also aims to drive change across the humanitarian system to better meet the needs of women and girls in emergencies. The United States is proud to lead the Call to Action in 2014.

Gender-based violence is a pervasive problem around the globe, and in order to effectively combat gender-based violence, USAID needs to work with a wide network of partners. Therefore, USAID will continue to address gender-based violence through partnerships with host governments, civil society organizations, universities, donor organizations, foundations and private companies.

Chairman Boxer, Ranking Member Paul, thank you once again for the opportunity to speak to this vitally important issue. I welcome your continued advice and counsel and would be pleased to take any questions you may have.

Senator BOXER. Thank you so much.

And before we turn to our other panelists, I would offer my good friend, Senator Durbin, who is the assistant majority leader, his 5 minutes, if he would like to take it.

STATEMENT OF HON. RICHARD J. DURBIN, U.S. SENATOR FROM ILLINOIS

Senator DURBIN. Thank you, Madam Chair. Thank you for your leadership on this issue, which has been acknowledged. I am sorry I missed our colleagues who were here on the first panel to dramatize the importance of this issue.

I struggle to understand why the United States has failed to pass the Convention on the Elimination of All Forms of Discrimination Against Women. But I understand politics. We have also failed to pass a convention dealing with disabilities, though we lead the world in our treatment and opportunity for people with disabilities. Time and again, I find the Senate is just unresponsive to taking formal action to acknowledge our responsibility and our leadership on issues.

But this is one that we just cannot ignore. What is happening to women across the world is well known and documented. I can recall years ago attending a speech by then-First Lady Hillary Clinton who had returned from a trip overseas, and she said something I have never forgotten. She said if I visit a developing country and I can only ask one question to determine what the future might be in that country, my question is how do you treat your women. That question and that answer will be a better insight into the opportunity for progress than almost any other question.

I have been over to the Democratic Republic of Congo several times. Sadly, it may hold the distinction of being the rape capital of the world because rape is used as a weapon of war there. And I visited the camps and met with many of the victims. It is an outrage.

And you wonder if there is anything that we in the West can do. Well, a number of us learned that what was fueling, in many instances, the economy in that part of the world was certain minerals that were being mined by slaves and sold. And so on a bipartisan basis, we tracked down those minerals and we came to learn sadly that many of us are carrying those minerals around with us every day.

So we established standards for accountability and transparency about where these minerals are being mined and under what circumstances and asked the companies that sell us the cell phones, as well as many other pieces of technology, to accept a corporate responsibility. Some said they would do it. Others said we will sue you, and so we are stuck in court on that basic question.

There are so many avenues here for us to follow and proceed down in terms of dealing with this issue, but bringing it to the attention of the public, as my friend and great writer, Nicholas Kristof, does almost on a weekly basis, is part of it.

Another part of it is to establish policies that are consistent with our goals as America's policies. One of them is the discouragement of child marriage, which was a provision that I added to a bill and ultimately became part of our law.

So I thank you for this hearing. I thank each of you for the work that you are doing. The United States has more that we can do, and on behalf of those who have no voice in the world, let us give them a voice here in Congress.

Thank you, Madam Chair.

Senator BOXER. Senator, thank you, and again, as Senator Murray was here and you were here, it just shows, I think, a real commitment to this issue on the part of the leadership. And I thank you.

So our first witness from what was going to be our last panel—but we will get all the statements in and then we will have a chance to question everyone—is Dr. Gary Barker, the international director of Promundo, a Brazilian-based NGO that works internationally to engage men and boys to promote gender equality and reduce violence against women. Dr. Barker has conducted extensive research on men, violence, gender, and health. He served as a consultant to numerous organizations, including the World Bank, the World Health Organization, the United Nations Development Program, and USAID.

Welcome, sir. Please proceed.

STATEMENT OF GARY BARKER, PH.D., INTERNATIONAL DIRECTOR, PROMUNDO, WASHINGTON, DC

Dr. BARKER. Thanks. Senator Boxer and other Senators, thank you for holding the event on this very important issue. I am thrilled to be able to talk about ways that we can engage men as part of the solution.

We heard before that these are not just a handful of horrific acts. We know from data, that we have globally, that 30 percent of the world's women will experience some form of violence from a man in their lifetime, most of the time men who they know.

What we do not say often enough is that we also know something about which men are using that violence, who are the men who are actually carrying this out, whether it is the men in India that you referenced at the beginning or men who carry out violence against a female partner in their home. We know something about them. In about 30,000 interviews that we have carried out in nearly 20 countries in a study carried out by Promundo and the International Center for Research on Women and the U.N., we have looked at which men are more likely to use violence.

First off, men who have seen their father carry this violence out against their mother are nearly two and a half times more likely to carry it out.

Men themselves who experience violence in the home or in the school, in the community are more likely to carry it out.

And what we see again and again and again is that about two-thirds of those men believe that other men around them think this violence is okay. In fact, they think nothing will happen to them if they use it. That does not mean they are worried about being arrested necessarily. They are not worried about being arrested. They are also not worried that the other men around them will say anything about it.

So we have something that is not just the behavior of a few bad men. We have something that is really ingrained in the silence of other men, how our systems do not react to it, how family members, as well as courts and teachers and everyone around, is watching this violence but not speaking out.

We talked a lot about the symptoms or rather the symptoms of this violence and the results of it, but we do not do enough to talk about these causes. And we think that if we look at the causes, we can figure out how we get to solutions.

Let me tell you first about a man in Brazil who we have worked with, Marcio. He is in a favela in Rio de Janiero. He is in a setting where he is one of those 40 percent of men who saw this violence growing up. He saw his father use this violence. And he said once he remembered distinctly his father came home, he was drunk, hit his mother. She was swollen. Her eye was swollen for a week. And he said my father's version of manhood was just that, having lots of women, drinking, parties. I never had presents. I never had him around. I had violence from him.

He talked about how it would be quite easy for him to repeat that violence. His anger about it, his inability to know other ways to interact with female partners. He came into Promundo's program and he was able to talk with other men about how to overcome similar situations. To look at Marcio now playing with his young son is to believe that change is possible. And our challenge now is how do we multiply that a million times over.

We start with the assumption that there is not enough prison space to lock up every man who has used violence. If we are talking about a behavior that a third of the world's men have carried out, we do not have enough prison space. Clearly we need to hold men accountable, but we need to think about what prevention looks like, how to take it seriously, and how to scale it up. And let me give you about five examples of how we think you can do that.

One is school-based work. We have spent a huge amount in the last years to get girls in school. Now we have to do this tremendous work of making schools safe for girls. We have done teacher training, including online teacher training, that we can scale up small-scale stuff to train 3,000 teachers in a year to reach up to 250,000 students. For a small amount, we can take the infrastructure we have invested in and see ways to scale up prevention.

Second, bystander intervention. We get men to follow the simple logic: you see something, say something. Speak out when you see your peers doing it, whether that is at the household level, your neighborhood, your neighbor. Groups like Breakthrough, Futures Without Violence, CARE, Promundo, and many others are doing this to say it is up to all of us men who are abhorred by this violence to speak out in the acts we see every day. You see your friend drunk harassing a girl, say something. You hear a politician harassing a Japanese politician, why do men not also speak out on that?

Third, we use the health sector. We know that a fifth of women will experience violence during pregnancy. We have spent a lot with the U.S. Government and others to make birthing safer for women. How do we also use that? We are working across four countries to train health care workers to reach men with activities around how to reduce couple conflict, how to be supportive fathers, and how to reduce violence from the very beginning. Again, we build on the services that are already there.

Fourth and finally, women's economic empowerment. The United States has invested a huge amount in microcredit programs, reaching up to 125 million women worldwide. We found that if we do a little bit of adding men to those processes, we can scale up the impact of that in terms of empowering women around autonomy and also reducing gender-based violence.

The point with all these is that with a small amount, $5 to $10, we can add on and scale up and build on the infrastructure we have already done to take prevention seriously.

Thank you.

[The prepared statement of Dr. Barker follows:]

PREPARED STATEMENT OF GARY BARKER, PH.D.

Honorable Chairwoman Boxer, Ranking Member Paul, and other members of the subcommittee, thank you for holding this hearing on such an important topic.

We all know by now the global extent of violence against women: An estimated 30 percent of women worldwide will experience physical or sexual violence from a man at some point in their lives, the majority of those husbands or partners or men they know. We have a growing body of evidence on the impact of this violence on women's and girls' lives, in terms of personal, political, economic, and health consequences. What we too often neglect is that we also know which men are more likely to use violence against women and girls.

From household surveys we and partners have carried out in more than 16 countries globally, we know that men who see their fathers or another man use violence are up to 2.5 times more likely to use violence against their wives or female partners. Men who themselves experienced violence in school, the home or the community are nearly twice as likely to use violence against women and girls. Men who witness and experience various kinds of violence growing up, and those who believe they are entitled to women's bodies are more likely to rape. Men who are displaced by conflict, men who are economically stressed, men who binge drink or drink excessively, and men who think their peers support their use of violence against women are also more likely to use violence against women.

The bottom line is that men who use violence against women have often witnessed or experienced violence in childhood, or have been socialized into believing that they are entitled to having power over women and girls. And they often have male peers who support them in their use of violence. This is not the behavior of a few bad men. It is part of the norms and attitudes about what it means to be men and women, and it is about how we raise our sons and daughters to see this violence as acceptable or not. The good news is that with this information, we know how to break cycles of violence against women.

Let me offer an example. I want to tell you about Marcio, a man from the favela of Santa Marta in Rio de Janeiro. Santa Marta is a setting where gang violence and violent response from the police against gangs has been chronic, where a third of parents use violence against children, where nearly half of children have witnessed a homicide, where men and women struggle to find adequate work and to provide for their families, and where a third of households have no adult man present at all. Marcio said this: "Once my father came home, he was drunk. He hit my mother. Her eye was swollen for a week. His version of manhood was just that: having lots of women, drinking, parties. I never had presents from my father, or him playing with me. I had this: violence and him abandoning us."

In group sessions that Promundo organized, Marcio told us about the pain and anger he felt in repeatedly witnessing that violence. He also talked about how he managed to avoid repeating the violence he saw around him: by talking about that pain, participating in a campaign and outreach activities that Promundo carried out in his community, and by finding other men like him working to break the violence. He told us: "Sharing my story with other men, I was able to overcome what I saw growing up. And I could help other men get over the violence they had seen too." Marcio is now a devoted father to a young son. To watch him interact with his son is to affirm that cycles of violence can be broken, to see that even men who witnessed this violence and experienced it can become supportive and nonviolent fathers and partners.

We start with the assumption that men who have used violence must be held accountable for that violence. But we also know that there is no way to lock up or imprison a third of the world's men. We must have functioning justice sectors, and committed individuals within them. Many of our partner organizations, such as Vital Voices and others, train members of the police and justice sectors, to take services and justice for victims seriously. But we must equally forcefully say this: we know that prevention works. We know how to end cycles of violence. And it's time to scale up the approaches that work. It's time for a bold vision to take what we know works to change attitudes, and to work with men and boys to break the cycle of violence against women and girls.

Let me offer a few examples:

First, we can train teachers and youth workers in carrying out school-based prevention models. In Brazil, we use online continuing education courses to instruct teachers in how to carry out group education with students about questioning the norms that underpin gender-based violence and gender inequality overall. In a year, we can reach more than 3,000 teachers, who in turn can reach more 250,000 students with a curriculum called Program H that calls young men and women to question the norms and attitudes that support inequality and violence. We have seen, as have other organizations doing this work, that such activities carried out with young people has the potential to shape and influence life-long attitudes about manhood and womanhood.

Second, we can scale up what we call bystander intervention programs, in which men, like Marcio and many others, can be trained how to speak out when they see other men condone or use violence. Via sports-based programming, on the soccer fields, and in locker rooms, Promundo, Futures without Violence, Sonke Gender Justice, Breakthrough and other organizations engage men and women in questioning the violence they see around them and appropriate ways to intervene. This is in effect the idea that if "you see something, you say something." You see your friend getting drunk and inappropriately harassing a young woman, and you speak out or offer help. You hear a man using violence, you speak out, you offer help, you make it known that it is not an acceptable behavior. You hear a public official use language condoning violence, you question it.

Third, we use the health sector to reach men, in particular via prenatal visits. We've seen that violence by men against women often goes up during pregnancy. In some of the settings we work in, up to one in five women experiences violence during pregnancy. We're working with partners and with the health sector, in a model called MenCare+, in Rwanda, Brazil, South Africa, and Indonesia to use prenatal visits as a place to both screen for violence and to recruit expectant fathers to prevent it. Specifically, we train health workers to carry out sessions with men on how to communicate better with their wives and partners, how to raise their children in nonviolent ways, and how to better understand their roles in maternal and child health. With this program, men are becoming more involved and less violent fathers. The expanded reach of prenatal services for women in countries around the world, gives us a tremendous opportunity and entry point; around 60–80 percent of fathers across countries are attending at least one prenatal appointment with their partners or wives. This interaction with the health system provides a key opportunity to engage men in doing their share of caregiving and to be involved fathers, as well as to reduce violence. And we use infrastructure that already exists.

Fourth, we can use the power and reach of economic empowerment programs for women. Microcredit and microfinance programs for women have been one of the success stories of international assistance and development. An estimated 125 million women are reached globally with these programs, many of those programs supported by USAID and other international donors. These programs work to give women income security and autonomy. At the same time some studies show that couple conflict can increase as women are economically empowered via such programs. Thus, we have seen that such programs can work even better if we use them as a space to recruit men via community outreach and group education with messages about couple cooperation and communication. When we have done this, we see that income gains are improved—that is women have even more income—couples cooperate more and couple conflict is reduced.

And finally, we're using the workplace as a space to reach men. To give an example, in Brazil we work with Petrobras, the national petroleum company, to encourage workers not to engage in sexual exploitation by having sex or paying for sex with underage girls. Of course this is against the law and men should not be doing so in first place, but we have carried out surveys in Brazil finding that 14 percent of men in the cities surveyed reported having paid for sex with a girl under the age of 18.

We know that this sexual exploitation often happens around spaces where lots of men are away from home. Petrobras and other employers ship men to various parts of the country to build new natural gas and petroleum installations, and too often, sexual exploitation comes along with that. Of course, Petrobras and others work with the Brazilian Government to hold accountable those who traffic young girls, but we think that's not enough. We carry out campaigns and training with human resources staff to promote discussions with the workers about why men pay for sex with underage girls. We work to create a culture in the workplace in which men question each other about this. At the beginning of these sessions, we'll hear men say things like this: "I paid for the party and drinks and she paid me back." At the end of the sessions, their peers will question this, speak out against it, and take those messages into bars and other spaces. In other words, we stop the demand before it happens while collaborating with the legal authorities to hold perpetrators accountable.

These approaches work. We have been able to evaluate impact, as partners have in many other settings, and we see changes in attitudes, and reductions in violence. Our challenge has been taking them to scale and sustaining them. Funding is too often inconsistent and short-term.

So what can the U.S. Government do? Consistent funding is necessary and IVAWA would be a key step toward that. In addition, the U.S. Government can look across its existing women's empowerment programs—economic empowerment; agriculture development; land title and legal rights initiatives; maternal, newborn, and child health programs; HIV prevention, workplace interventions and others—and find ways to add approaches for reaching men to its existing initiatives. We can build on the existing infrastructure and existing large-scale programs to engage men with these approaches. In no way should this prevention work with men take away from the existing work to empower women economically and socially. It can and should be part of integrated prevention efforts. We have consistently found that if we use this existing infrastructure—in schools, the health sector, the workplace or sports-based programming—we can reach men and boys for as little as $5–$10 per beneficiary in some settings.

We stand by colleagues around the world who call for ending the impunity that surrounds men's use of violence against women and girls. But punishing perpetrators is not enough. Two weeks ago in London, the U.S. took a lead with others in calling for ending impunity around sexual violence in conflict. But that call and too many others like it do not go far enough in saying what we know works to prevent violence against women, including sexual violence, from happening in the first place. It is not enough only to hold accountable the perpetrators. We need to reach all the boys and men, like Marcio, who witness and experience violence, to break cycles of violence—to create a generation of boys and men who do not use nor believe in using violence of any kind against women and girls. And we know how to do it.

Senator BOXER. Thank you.

Women cannot do this alone. We cannot. And I would say without the men in the Senate—and Barbara Mikulski, before a lot of women came here, used to call them the Sir Galahads of the Senate. This is a partnership, full-out. So thank you for all your work.

So now we are going to turn to Hauwa Ibrahim. She is the senior partner at the Aries Law Firm in Nigeria. Throughout her career, Ms. Ibrahim has devoted herself to advancing women's rights in Nigeria and is best known for her work defending women in northern Nigeria's sharia courts. She was also recently selected to serve on the Presidential commission established by Nigerian President Goodluck Jonathan to investigate the abduction of more than 200 girls from a boarding school in northern Nigeria.

We are very honored to have you here. Please proceed.

STATEMENT OF HAUWA IBRAHIM, SENIOR PARTNER, ARIES LAW FIRM, NIGERIA

Ms. IBRAHIM. Thank you so much, Madam Chair, and thank you, other members. My gratitude knows no bounds. This is an honor and this is a privilege to speak about combating violence against women as a responsibility of our common humanity beyond just women.

I was born and raised in northern Nigeria. I became educated by accident, and I became a lawyer by accident. I guess I went to teach at Harvard for 3 years by accident. But it is some of this accident that I have written about in a longer testimony. And if you do not mind, let me speak from my heart.

Senator BOXER. Yes. We will put the testimony in the record. Please proceed.

Ms. IBRAHIM. So I will just speak about a few issues from my heart to you.

I may murder English because English is my fifth language, and I never learnt it in the classroom.

I have been a lawyer for 20 years, like you mentioned. Over 20 years, I have practiced law in sharia courts. I have been defending women sentenced to death by stoning in northern Nigeria, and as of recent, I just came back 2 days ago from Nigeria and I will speak a little bit about what is happening with this Boko Haram and the Chibok girls.

So on the 6th of May, the President appointed me by name. I am the only member appointed by name to serve on this fact finding committee. And the past 6 weeks have been eventful. A lot of what we have found out and what we have written—it is in written testimony and it is classified. So I am not going to speak about it. But I will speak about to a few things that are public.

I came back with a heavy heart, but I am glad to be here to address the issue of gender-based violence, which is what this is all about, the kidnapping of the Chibok girls. Let me say that with the full cooperation of the Nigerian community, we were able to find out a lot of information as to where those girls may be.

But let me just put out some figures out here. There has been a kidnapping. Over 300 girls have been kidnapped; 119 girls escaped from their kidnappers; 217 are still remaining, and in the past couple of weeks, 57 have also escaped. Sadly, we have 219 girls still unaccounted for and they are with their captors living in a semi-hell.

Our committee met with grieving parents of the escaped girls of Chibok. There is a dire situation of security in northern Nigeria, especially in the City of Borno. Boko Haram seems to be waxing stronger. They are a threat to peace and security in our region and beyond.

But why Boko Haram, and why is this kidnapping happening even today? There are three reasons I want to mention here. Boko Haram—so far we have found out they have been very smart and they are well organized. They have more sophisticated arms. And with respect, I want to say that this is something that is heavy in my heart. The arms that are out there are so unnecessary—they create more violence, especially are gender-based violence. There are issues that have to do with motivation on both sides, first, on the Boko Haram, on the other side, Nigerian security that hopefully, in a bigger picture, we will address in the future.

But let me say that one of the challenges we found on the ground is the issue of food security. We also realize that there is a forest called Sambisa and there is a mountain called Mandara Mountains where the Boko Haram will be camping. And hopefully, with the assistance of the United States and the international community, we will be able to surmount some of these difficulties of finding where they are and slowing them down, especially creating in a bigger picture of global peace and security.

What is the way forward? I believe engaging them and collaboration could be one way. Getting back our girls is something that is very dear to our hearts. It is more of a collective interest. It is beyond north versus south or Christian versus Muslim. It is beyond our greed and our corruption. It is more about engaging women, especially mothers, sisters, grandmothers, and aunts. Today is day number 71 that the girls have been with their kidnappers. It is 1 day too many.

Let me speak briefly about the United States as a city on a hill and a beacon of hope for all of us. I was in Jordan last week, and what I have to show for this is a broken ankle. But we had 17 countries that were represented, Madam Chair, and for all the 17 countries that have spoken, the United States was mentioned and was mentioned positively. So may I say that you are, indeed, a beacon of hope and a city on the hill. And I hope that that is taken seriously.

The passing of CEDAW and the IVAWA, if that is done, will lead to a partnership in our work and it will make our workload easier. It will help in our economic activities.

My time is up and I want to conclude by saying that northern Nigeria has been hidden in isolation, sometimes self-imposed. The land is bleeding. There is much distrust. Recently, the parents of the Chibok girls have been suffering with high blood pressure. Two of them have died in the past few weeks. No to violence against women is what I stand here to say, and no to all form of control of a woman's body. But we hope that we have partners in you and friends as we believe that we will rise again, and I believe that the sun will shine again. And with your help and commitment, we will get the girls back.

A powerful force unites us in this room, irrespective of the sex or color of our skin or our religious affiliation or our creed or our privileges. My hope today, and it will so remain, is that there is a powerful force that binds us and that is our common humanity. That is the dignity of all of us. And with that, we hope with the passage of CEDAW and IVAWA in the United States, the world will be a better place for generations to come.

Thank you.

[The prepared statement of Ms. Ibrahim follows:]

PREPARED STATEMENT OF HAUWA IBRAHIM

I want to begin with my sincere appreciation for this invitation to testify before your subcommittee this morning not only because of the recent tragedies in northern Nigeria but also because of my longstanding commitment to combating discrimination and gender based violence on an International scale. My presence here is meaningful not simply because I have the opportunity to speak on behalf of the "Chibok girls"—but more so, because serendipity and age are the only two things that distinguish me from the 219 still missing girls. I was born and lived most of my life in Gombe state in northern Nigeria. I was a child in a poor family and raised in a Muslim home. As was the local practice, I was given away in marriage at age 10. Being the "stubborn" child in my family, at 11 I ran away from home to a boarding school for girls. My family told me not to come back but I was determined to get an education. I eventually became a lawyer—the first women from my state and returned there to practice law. However, since the courts in northern Nigeria use sharia law women were not allowed to speak, so I had to pass notes to male lawyers to represent my clients, including women sentenced to death by stoning for adultery. Most of my cases were pro bono helping women and children gain justice primarily through informal negotiations outside the courts. Today I am a visiting lecturer at Harvard University but all this happened accidentally. The life situation of the kidnapped schoolgirls, who are most likely enduring living hell, is one for which my empathy and concern is boundless.

On April 14, Boko Haram came to Chibok with the intention of kidnapping the girls. To distract attention from this nefarious purpose, the Boko Haram first attacked the village and a nearby military base. They arrived at the school at 11:45 at night, the girls were all in bed and the men had official uniforms and trucks and buses. They told the girls that Boko Haram was about to attack the school and they should leave with them. Then they proceeded to steal all the food and kitchen equipment and burn down the school. This is how Boko Haram operates. As has been reported, there were 330 girls boarding at the school in order to take the national exam for higher education; 219 of these girls are still missing; 130 boys also took exams at the school but did not board overnight. I am serving on the President's Commission along with government representatives and representatives of other nongovernmental organizations. I was one of the few people appointed by name as a result of my experience of living and working in the North, helping women in the community to secure justice under shariah law.

In order to fully understand the situation of the kidnapping of the Chibok girls, it is important to note the vast differences between the southern and northern parts of Nigeria. The South has benefited from development and local resources with infrastructure and modernization, including a greater public role for women. Girls receive an education and while challenges persist, the opportunities for a girl growing up in the South are vastly different than in the North. Though I don't have exact figures, I can report that the majority of boys in the North receive an education but the proportion of girls in school is precious few. Girls are expected to marry young and as I was told at home, "The heaven for a woman is at your husband's feet." That is partly why these girls and their families were so determined to take the national exam which is the gateway to higher education. And that is also why I have been determined to use the opportunities and education that I have received to help the people in the region, particularly women and girls.

Violence against these girls, against women, and our children, is simply unacceptable. I am glad and hopeful, as the United States has not left the issue unresolved.

Both in response to our own hearts and minds that refuse to accept violence against the kidnapped girls and to the mourning and grief of the girls' families and friends, the United States has continued and will hopefully continue to fight against violence and for peace. Especially the comprehensive leadership by the United States to support efforts to build the capacity of local women's and other human rights organizations to fight violence against women and girls by committing financial resources to such efforts. Future joint efforts by the international community should not simply fight violence—they should insist on full transparency, accountability and willingness to share intelligence, and uphold integrity of budgetary decisions.

Beyond the scope of the Chibok kidnapping, the northern region of Nigeria is undergoing its toughest moments, with over 70 percent youth unemployment, widespread abject poverty, desolation, and hopelessness. In adverse situations, religion and religious extremism become dangerous opium to the hopeless. It is clear that perverse religious indoctrination by Boko Haram, among others, is anything but Islamic. We have seen atrocities. We have witnessed horrific incidences, slaughtering of fellow human beings in the name of doing God's work. We are shocked by this high-scale destruction and perverse terrorism. We have grieved at the loss of loved ones. A situation where the abducted girls were separated from their parents, friends and love ones as well as from their religion has no place in Islam. In fact, the Quran 2:56 says ''There shall be no compulsion in religion.''

Against the various issues that we as an international community face, one goal we can support and reinforce is that of reduced violence. Amongst the various types of violence that undermine stability today, gender-based violence has yet to be freed from the shackles of silence and suppression. The recent kidnapping of over 200 girls in Chibok, Borno State, in northeastern Nigeria illustrated the scale of such gender-based violence and prompted a global call for action. Who is better suited for such a call to action than the United States of America? I believe that, as a city upon a hill and a beacon of hope, the United States has the full capability of combating the recent rising tide of violence against women both domestically and internationally. And it is not only myself that sees the United States as a city upon a hill—throughout a meeting with people from 17 countries in Amman, Jordan, last week at the invitation of HRH, Prince El-Hassan Bin Talal, no single moment passed without a positive reference to the United States.

In looking forward to long-term peace and stability, the various countries interested in peace and freedom should invest in cooperative technology pooling. Furthermore, the dire deficiency of manpower and appropriate counterterrorist training were both key issues during the Chibok kidnapping, and I believe that directing resources and funding toward military training and personnel recruitment (especially in countries facing such high terrorist activity) will reinforce stability and global peace.

I also believe that at the local level in Nigeria our human resources could be better used to stop the violence. When members of a village unite toward one cause, the commitment and love put forth by each individual member become a force to be highly reckoned with. I believe that, just as local intelligence and reliance on other local means of counterterrorism such as the civilian Joint Task Forces (JTF), comprising hunters, fishermen, cow rearers, should be fully utilized in future pursuits of stability and peace, establishing a communal safety net that would focus on the correct upbringing and teaching of children would both mitigate current insurgency manpower and principles and limit future influence of fundamentalist indoctrination.

Yet while even a single candle can defy the surrounding darkness, the international community has a rising sun and beacon of hope. While I believe that combating gender-based violence should not end with just the passing of IVAWA and CEDAW, which I believe is sorely needed, the leadership of the United States in ensuring the passing of the International Violence Against Women Act (IVAWA) and the ratification of CEDAW will undeniably pave a smoother path for future work against violence and will certainly make our hands-on work lighter. I strongly believe that ratification by the United States will make the treaty stronger and give it a higher status that will provide a greater incentive for Nigeria and other countries to make a more serious effort to end discrimination and violence against women and girls.

That though it looks dark and hopeless, and we are grieved by our inabilities to get the girls back, we will not give up, the sun will rise again, may be, even brighter.

Senator BOXER. Thank you for your eloquence. And I could not agree with you more on the action items on your list.

So finally, we are pleased to have Ms. Jacqueline O'Neill, the director of the Institute for Inclusive Security, an organization dedicated to demonstrating and supporting women's contribution to peace-building all over the world. Ms. O'Neill consults regularly with NATO and other multilateral organizations. She has also designed training for police, military, and civilian professionals. Previously she served at the United Nations mission in Sudan and as a policy advisor to Canada's Secretary of State for Asia-Pacific.

And we are grateful for the wealth of knowledge and breadth of experience that our panel members have. All of them and that includes you, Ms. O'Neill. So please let us hear from you.

STATEMENT OF JACQUELINE O'NEILL, DIRECTOR, INSTITUTE FOR INCLUSIVE SECURITY, WASHINGTON, DC

Ms. O'NEILL. Chairman Boxer, you are known around the world for shining a spotlight on these issues. I want to thank you, Ranking Member Paul, Chairman Menendez, Ranking Member Corker, and the other members.

For the last 15 years, Inclusive Security has increased the inclusion of women in peace and security processes around the world. All that we do is driven by the over 3,000 members of our global Women Waging Peace Network, many of whom, Senator Boxer, you have hosted here in Congress.

This network includes women like those recently displaced by war in South Sudan who, earlier this year, despite living in camps literally partitioned in half with a line separating two tribes, began crossing the divide at first to talk over tea in each other's tents and then to organize a joint march to the governor's house, most walking barefoot for hours in the sun, to demand an end to the violence and a voice in the process.

Our network also includes Zainab Bangura, whose father threw her out of the house in Sierra Leone at age 12 because she refused to marry. Zainab's mother left with her and somehow provided her an education. Zainab went on to become her country's Foreign Minister and now travels the world as the top U.N. envoy on sexual violence in conflict. This near child bride from a once war-torn nation told me a few weeks ago, "I say to those men who kidnapped the girls in Nigeria what I say to all men who rape. Whoever you are, wherever you are, we will run after you. And we will find you."

My written submission echoes many of the points that my remarkable fellow witnesses have made this morning. So in the spirit of compelling action, I want to focus directly on two priorities that we see as transformative but generally underattended.

Senator BOXER. We will put your full statement in the record.

Ms. O'NEILL. Thank you.

So the first is that we absolutely must get more women to participate directly in more peace negotiations. It is often at this stage that the most troubled countries lay the foundation for their future. As one woman said to me recently, "If we're not at the table, you can be sure we're on the menu."

About 92 percent of those who negotiated peace agreements in the last 40 years were men. The result is that half of all peace agreements collapse within 5 years, and the vast majority fail to address the topic of sexual violence in conflict.

Evidence shows that, when present, women raise these issues, but they often broaden the discussion even further, moving beyond who gets to run which ministry and where borders are divided, to address the underlying drivers of conflict and, importantly, to reduce the structural barriers that contribute to violence and discrimination.

In Guatemala, for example, women ensured that talks addressed police power. In Darfur, women spoke about food security. In Northern Ireland, they raised integrated education.

The single most important policy tool that the U.S. Government has to increase women's participation at peace talks is its National Action Plan on Women, Peace, and Security. The plan is being rolled out, but progress is much too slow. And Congress can help speed up its implementation.

First, by passing the bipartisan Women, Peace, and Security Act, which you, Senator Boxer, and others have championed, and second, by holding a hearing about the National Action Plan to which you would invite the Secretaries of Defense, State, and the Administrator of USAID to talk about progress, gaps, and how they are working together.

The second major priority to which I want to call your attention relates to women's roles in security forces. The numbers here are dismal. In Pakistan, for example, women make up less than 1 percent of the police force. Without a doubt, access to protection and justice for survivors of sexual violence increases when women are meaningfully integrated into security forces. Females are simply far more likely to report cases of assault to other women.

But again, the value that women bring is much broader. They contribute to all aspects of mission success and effectiveness and, when present in large enough numbers, can transform institutions and the public's perception of power, force, and legitimacy.

Women's recruitment, retention, and safety in security forces are woefully underresourced, and Congress can change this too. Last year, Congress took action on this issue for the first time ever, appropriating $25 million for this purpose in Afghanistan. A week ago, thanks to the support from many on this subcommittee, the Senate Appropriations Committee passed its foreign operations appropriations bill which included provisions prioritizing the same thing for Pakistan's police force. Members can ensure that the final bill retains these provisions and that funding is at least maintained this year for women in the Afghan National Security Forces in any defense spending and authorization bills.

I will stop here so we can turn to questions.

[The prepared statement of Ms. O'Neill follows:]

PREPARED STATEMENT OF JACQUELINE O'NEILL

Chairman Boxer, you're known around the world for shining a spotlight on these issues. Thanks to you, Ranking Member Paul, Chairman Menendez, Ranking Member Corker, and members of the subcommittee. Thank you as well to all in civil society here and abroad who play such an important role in provoking change.

For the last 15 years, The Institute for Inclusive Security, led by Ambassador Swanee Hunt, has increased the inclusion of women in peace and security processes. We work on current conflicts, in countries affected by war, and with policymakers in the U.S., other governments, NATO, the U.N., and beyond.

All that we do is driven by the over 3,000 members of our global Women Waging Peace Network.

The Network includes women like those recently displaced by war in South Sudan, who earlier this year, despite living in camps literally partitioned in half—with a line separating two tribes—began crossing the divide. At first to share stories over tea in each other's tents, and then to organize a joint march to the governor's house—most walking barefoot for hours under a blazing sun—to demand an end to the violence and a voice in the process.

The Network includes female police officers like some in Pakistan, who face harassment from their colleagues at work and isolation from their families at home, yet proudly button up their uniforms each morning because they feel a call to serve.

It also includes Zainab Bangura, whose father threw her out of their house in Sierra Leone at age 12 because she refused to marry. Zainab's mother left with her, and somehow provided her daughter with an education. Zainab went on to become her country's Foreign Minister and now travels the world as the top U.N. envoy on sexual violence in conflict. This near child bride from a once war-torn nation told me a few weeks ago, ''I say to those men who kidnapped the girls in Nigeria what I say to all men who rape: Whoever you are, wherever you are, we will run after you. And we will find you.''

Zainab and others will agree that if there is any good news in the fight against violence and discrimination, it's this: We have not yet fully engaged the single greatest resource available—women themselves.

To a dramatic and disgraceful extent, women continue to be excluded from essential areas of decisionmaking. They are not yet full and equal partners in developing and maintaining the elements of society that most directly impact their ability to live free from violence and discrimination.

Women's full security requires effective governance, where just laws are applied equally and there is equity in access to services and opportunities. It requires access to justice, which relies not only on a well-functioning judiciary and legal system, but also on effective and representative police and other security forces. Women's security requires their participation in defining the future of their state—as formal decisionmakers and as contributors to public discourse.[1] Fundamentally, it also requires widespread acceptance of the dignity and value of all persons.

We will see a significant shift in all forms of violence and discrimination when—and only when—we recognize women as fundamental actors in every one of those areas.

How do we do this? What can Congress do? The range of actions required is broad; let me call to your attention two priorities that are transformative, but underattended.

PEACE NEGOTIATIONS

First, we absolutely must get more women to participate directly in more peace negotiations.

It's often at this stage that the most troubled countries lay the foundation for their future. As one woman said to me recently, ''If we're not at the table, you can be sure we're on the menu.''

About 92 percent of the people who have negotiated peace agreements in the last 40 years were men.[2] The result? Half of all peace agreements collapse within their first 5 years, and the vast majority fail to address the issue of sexual violence in conflict, the topic of the major global conference hosted last week in the U.K.

Only 18 out of 300 peace accords signed since 1989, and only three cease-fire agreements in all of recorded history, have mentioned sexual violence.

Evidence shows that, when present, women raise this issue. But they often broaden the discussion even further, moving the conversation beyond who gets to run which ministry and where borders are set, to address the underlying drivers of conflict and reduce the structural barriers that contribute to violence and discrimination.

In Guatemala, for example, women ensured that talks addressed police power. In Darfur, women spoke about food security. In Northern Ireland, they raised integrated education.

Women's exclusion not only jeopardizes the sustainability of an agreement; it condemns women to struggle even harder for representation and justice later on.

The single most important policy tool the U.S. Government has to increase women's participation at peace talks is its National Action Plan on Women, Peace, and Security. Launched via Executive order in 2011, it's a whole-of-government strategy whose goal is simple but profound: to ensure that women are equal partners in preventing conflict and building peace.

The Action Plan is being rolled out, but progress is much too slow. Congress can speed up its implementation.

First, by passing the bipartisan Women, Peace, and Security Act which Senators Boxer, Kirk, and others in both Chambers and on both sides of the aisle have championed. This bill would strengthen the ability of Congress to oversee implementation of the National Action Plan and coordinate the funding that has already been employed to resource it.

Second, by holding a hearing about the National Action Plan. Members could invite the Secretaries of Defense and State and the Administrator of USAID to speak about how far their organizations have come, how far they still need to go, and how they're working together.

Third, by keeping the Nation Action Plan foremost in the minds of the nation's leaders. Imagine if every potential appointee to a position of influence in diplomacy, defense, or development was asked at a confirmation hearing how the principles of the Plan are reflected in his or her priorities. Even the fear simply of being caught without an answer would prompt meaningful reflection and preparation by candidates and agencies that support them.

Fourth, by ensuring that every congressional delegation, particularly those to regions most affected by war and violence against women, make a point of meeting with local women leaders from civil society and government to signal their importance and hear from them directly.

SECURITY FORCES

The second priority to which I want to draw your attention relates to women's roles in security forces.

The numbers here are dismal. In Pakistan, women make up less than 1 percent of the police force. In Afghanistan, they're less than a third of 1 percent of the National Army. Worldwide, women are only about 10 percent of police. In the Middle East and North Africa, that average is 2 percent. At the U.N., only 3 percent of military and 10 percent of police personnel are women. Even in the U.S., women make up only about 20 percent of today's military.

While policies and practices are shifting slowly, in the U.S. and around the world there is absurd foot dragging when it comes to recognizing that women's full and meaningful involvement in police, military, and other services fundamentally increases the effectiveness of those forces and their ability to serve and protect men, women, boys, and girls.

Without a doubt, access to protection and justice for survivors of sexual violence increases when women are meaningfully integrated into security forces. Females are simply far more likely to report cases of assault to other women. Data from 39 countries show that when women police officers are present, there are significantly higher rates of reporting.[3]

But the value of women in security forces is much broader. They contribute to all aspects of mission success and, when present in large enough numbers, can transform institutions and the public's perception of power, force, and legitimacy.

Women's recruitment, retention, and safety in security forces are woefully underresourced. Congress can change this.

It's time to redefine the purpose for which the U.S. spends billions of dollars on security assistance. U.S. support should, in large part, be dedicated to the development of inclusive, representative, and professional forces—ones that reflect the makeup of the populations they're tasked to serve.

Being explicit about goals also means being explicit about money. Policy priorities need to be resourced with specific appropriations for the recruitment, retention, and safety of women in police and militaries. Last year, Congress did this for the first time ever, appropriating $25 million for this purpose in Afghanistan.[4]

A week ago, thanks to support from many on this subcommittee, the Senate Appropriations Committee passed its Foreign Operations Appropriations bill, which included provisions prioritizing the same for women in Pakistan's police force. The bill even recognized the importance of recruiting more women into security forces to combat gender-based violence. Again, for the first time ever.

Members of this subcommittee can continue to demonstrate leadership by ensuring the final bill retains these provisions and by at least maintaining funding this year for women in the Afghan National Security Forces in any defense spending and authorization bills.

CONCLUSION

It's beyond time to recognize that not only are violence and discrimination against women an affront to our collective humanity; they're also a threat to our collective security.

Harvard researcher Valerie Hudson recently analyzed 174 countries and found that the best predictor of a state's peacefulness is not its level of wealth, its level of democracy, or its ethnoreligious identity; it's how well its women are treated. The larger the gender gap, the more likely a state is to be involved in violent conflict—inside and outside of its borders.[5]

In London last week, the Chief of the Australian Army spoke about sexual violence in conflict and the choice to be a protector or a perpetrator. He said there is no third option, no bystanders, explaining, "The standard you walk past is the standard you accept."

Thank you for trying to stop us in our tracks.

End Notes

[1] Barsa, Michelle. "Progress or Peril: The Role for Women in Defining Afghanistan's Future." Presentation, Women's Foreign Policy Group, Washington, DC, June 5, 2014.

[2] U.N. Women (October 2012). "Women's Participation in Peace Negotiations: Connections Between Presence and Influence." (NY: UN Women), 3.

[3] U.N. Women (2011). "2011–2012 Progress of the World's Women: In Pursuit of Justice." (NY: U.N. Women), 59.

[4] The Fiscal Year 2014 National Defense Authorization Act and Consolidated Appropriations Act reserved no less than $25 million of the Afghanistan Security Forces Fund for the recruitment, retention, and security of women in the Afghan National Security Forces.

[5] Hudson, V.; Ballif-Spanvill, B.; Caprioli, M.; & Emmett, C. (2012). "Sex and World Peace." (NY: Columbia University Press), 205.

Senator BOXER. Thank you. I have a number of questions. So I am just going to keep going until I have to go to vote. So we will just get started.

Ms. Markham, many of us know the story of Malala Yousafzai, a brave Pakistani school girl and outspoken advocate for girls' education who was nearly killed in a brutal attack by Taliban gunmen. And I introduced the Malala Yousafzai Scholarship Act. The bill would expand an existing USAID scholarship program to ensure that 50 percent of the scholarships awarded go to women. Not an outrageous request. Previously, only a quarter of the recipients had been women. So our bill says, no, you must do 50 percent.

Now, my bill has not yet been enacted, but USAID committed to providing 50 percent of new scholarships under this program to women, which is great. But I was disappointed to learn that only 29 percent of the scholarships that have been awarded in the first half of 2014 have been for women. Does USAID really plan to award at least 50 percent of all scholarships to women? I think it is critical that I know now because I do not like hearing you are going to do it and then you do not do it. So what is the story there?

Ms. MARKHAM. Thank you for that question.

As you know, we have been working across a wide range of programs in Pakistan to make sure that girls and young women are involved in the schools. And I believe that the delay has been the fact that we are in between school years just now and in the fall we will reach the 50 percent of scholarships provided, including the Fulbright Program.

In addition——

Senator BOXER. When you say the fall, when will you be able to confirm that for me?

Ms. MARKHAM. I will have to check with my colleagues in the Pakistan office, but in this briefing, they said that in the first half we had not reached it but that we were fully intending to.

Senator BOXER. But you said the fall.

Ms. MARKHAM. Yes. Where are we now? We are in June. So in the coming months, we will know as they enroll.

Senator BOXER. So let us just be clear that I will call you on October 1.

Ms. MARKHAM. I look forward to that call.

Senator BOXER. Okay, good.

In your testimony, you highlight a number of important USAID programs that prevent and respond to violence against women from the Safe School pilot program in Ghana to a health care provider training program in Haiti. But I am not clear whether the programs you discuss fit within a comprehensive, targeted approach to ending violence against women. You are doing some really good things. Are they part of an overall plan? is my question.

Ms. MARKHAM. So we do believe that all of our gender-based violence programs need to have a multisectoral approach, whether it is economic development, education, health care. Even infrastructure issues have to be taken into account to respond to gender-based violence. Some are more specifically focused. For instance, in the Democratic Republic of Congo where violence against women is so overwhelming, a lot of the programs are more focused on that. But even in the Safe Schools program, even in economic or micro-enterprise programs, we try to combat gender-based violence and address the root causes of the gender imbalance which causes this. Haiti is actually a great example. It is going to be our first mission where gender-based violence is integrated across all programs. So whether it is water, education, health care, even governance programs, gender-based violence will be a part of it. In other places where the need is more acute, the gender-based violence takes more of a lead and those other sectors support that work instead of the other way around.

Senator BOXER. Thank you.

Ambassador Russell, the International Violence Against Women Act is so critical because we want to codify in law the existing Office of Global Women's Issues within the State Department and the Ambassador at Large for Global Women's Issues. It would also require the implementation of a U.S. global strategy to prevent and respond to violence against women and girls, including the development of comprehensive, individual country plans for 5 to 20 countries, which I think is critical because different countries will have different problems and issues. And I am just asking you a very basic question. I think it will not be hard for you to answer. But will you commit to working with me to enact IVAWA?

Ambassador RUSSELL. Yes.

Senator BOXER. That is good.

Ambassador RUSSELL. Senator, you know when I was here working in the Senate, I worked on that bill, and I think I was the first staff person to work on it. I care so much about it. And I think, importantly, I really believe in the approach of the bill. I think it is critically important to approach it that way, comprehensively.

And I also think we have tried to do, from the administration's perspective, what we can setting up my position, Susan's position, trying to approach these issues that way. But Congress—you all weighing in on this is an incredibly powerful statement not unlike what you did here this morning. And I think you cannot underestimate the power that will have in the world. And I think doing that would make it——

Senator BOXER. I know you have a lot of connections here in the Senate. So if people you know are not on this bill, please get them on the bill.

I want to talk about CEDAW, the Convention on the Elimination of All Forms of Discrimination Against Women, because I feel if you just stopped someone in the street who was not that into all of our nuances here and said, can you believe that America is standing with countries like Sudan, Somalia, and Iran where 187 countries have already ratified this, they would be horrified. And so does the administration support the ratification of CEDAW?

Ambassador RUSSELL. Yes. And I would say this. In a way, it is somewhat easier for people in the United States to take it for granted because our laws are so progressive here. But I will say when I travel around the world, it is a lifeline for women, and they are desperate for us to pass it because they do not understand why we have not. And in their countries, people look to the United States and people who are opposed to it in their countries say, you know, look, the United States has not passed that. And that is a very challenging thing. My colleague here is saying yes, that is true. It is very confusing for people, and I think it really undermines our efforts and it deprives us of a very powerful tool. It is a very conflicting statement. And I think this concept of us as a beacon of hope is a powerful image, and it is very important to these countries and to the advocates in those countries. And we should not underestimate the power of that image.

Senator BOXER. Well, I think it is important that everyone within the sound of my voice knows that this administration strongly supports CEDAW——

Ambassador RUSSELL. Yes, we do.

Senator BOXER [continuing]. And the International Violence Against Women Act. In trying to explain it to folks, I would explain it this way. It is internal politics and it is ludicrous. And it is side issues that have nothing to do with the basic message, which is equality.

Ambassador RUSSELL. It is confusing to people.

Senator BOXER. It is confusing to people, but I think if you say to people it is politics, it is internal politics. It is not a rejection of the notion that we are all created equal. But it is extremely frustrating nonetheless and ridiculous. It should be a nonissue. And we will keep on pushing.

And my last question for you, Ambassador. Last month, we were horrified to learn that two young girls in India were murdered after being brutally raped. Tragically attacks against women are all too common in India.

And so I wrote to India's newly elected Prime Minister urging him to take immediate action to combat violence and improve the safety and security of women and girls.

Ambassador Russell, you traveled to India in February to discuss efforts by Indian police to protect women from violence and abuse. Can you kind of give us a report of where you think things stand there?

Ambassador RUSSELL. I can. Obviously, the stories of the gang rape, the hangings are absolutely horrifying. The interesting thing is that the Indian public had a very strong reaction to that as well, and I think the politicians there are responding. It will be very interesting to see how the new Prime Minister reacts to this, and we are hopeful that there will be a positive and forward-thinking reaction.

We are engaged in a dialogue with the Indian Government, a women's empowerment dialogue. That has been ongoing. We are in the process of negotiating an MOU with the Indian Government on women's issues, and I think that we are fairly optimistic going forward. We have been talking to them about gender-based violence issues in places that we can share experiences with them. And so at this point, I am somewhat hopeful that this will be a positive effort going forward.

Obviously, we are waiting to see how this government reacts to those, but we will certainly keep in touch with you on that. I know that you have a tremendous interest in it, and we certainly do as well.

Senator BOXER. Please, and I would be very happy to help as well.

Ambassador RUSSELL. That would be terrific.

Senator BOXER. Now, Mr. Barker—I should say Dr. Barker—I am so proud of your work. And it has occurred to me over many years now that clearly there is some kind of an advantage that men in these countries get—boys and men who commit this violence. And if we could just have an ethos around the world that said real men do not beat up women, real men protect women. I would also add real men vote for women. [Laughter.]

So we need to get that ethos out there in a pretty strong way. You are a weakling if you attack a woman. You do not stand for anything. You are low. But if you protect a woman, you are really a special human being.

It seems to me in this day and age of the ability to get messages out—have you thought about, for example, recruiting men who are looked up to in the sports world? Have you done that? Can we do more of that? Because I believe that is the most effective way— when you have these real role models saying, no, no, no, no. This is not how you become a real man. So talk to me about that and whether sports can play a role in your work.

Dr. BARKER. Well, it happens to be the World Cup going on at the moment. So it is a great moment to talk about sports and getting men on the right page.

I absolutely echo your sentiment that what we are trying to do is get the message out and we print this on T-shirts in English and kiswahili and Kenya, Rwanda, and Portuguese which says men of quality are not afraid of equality. So trying to use a message that, yes, men should vote for women. We have four women Presidents in the Americas region. We have yet to have one here, but who knows what happens in a couple of years.

So part of this whole change is that, how do——

Senator BOXER. Meet me afterward and we will talk about it. [Laughter.]

Dr. BARKER. I would be glad to.

Senator BOXER. Some interesting possibilities.

Dr. BARKER. We are very much trying to tap into that. How do you use the sports field as a place to say we can change these norms? And there are a lot of men out there in silence who already are appalled by this violence. So it is not like we have got to start a new movement. What we are trying to do is make it safe for men to say we expect you to speak out. You have been harmed by this violence. You have seen it. Say something about it.

We have got some public service announcements running at the moment in Brazil around the World Cup. We have a soccer player, football player putting his name out on the issue of the sexual exploitation of underage girls. We have done household data in Brazil that finds about 14 percent of men acknowledge they have ever paid for sex with a girl under the age of 18. That, of course, is illegal in Brazil. Lots of efforts to do the law enforcement side. But to say, wait a minute, as we put their stories out, as we put what they say to justify it out, most men are appalled by that. And so, again, the message is getting football players, getting fathers, getting men everywhere to say we do not agree with this. And there are a lot of men who are already resonating to it. So we are doing the public service announcements but also trying to take it to where guys hang out every day, the locker room, schools, after-school programs, so all of the above.

Senator BOXER. Well, I just want to say anything that we can do here to help, the women of the Senate, the men of the Senate that care so much about this—we have people who are role models to young men and they happen to be other men who are successful in the areas of sports and other very highlighted professions. I just think in my heart that could turn the tide. It really could turn the tide because it is not only a question of the right thing to do, but if you do the wrong thing, that is not really being a man. And I think that is something that has been on my mind for so long and how to do that.

I am a mom of a son and a daughter, and I am a grandmother of a little girl and little boys. So for me, their future really depends on the fact that we need to have zero tolerance for violence of any kind against anyone, any religion, any color, anything. There is no tolerance for violence. Zero. So I think the people who are the most respected in society out there—you know, we need to tap into that. So anything I can do to help.

Ms. Ibrahim, I just want to ask you—when we heard about the girls, the audacity of hundreds of girls being kidnapped, it shook this country. It shook us. And I wonder in your country did it shake people up or was it more or less, oh, there they go again? Can you give me a sense of the truth about that?

Ms. IBRAHIM. It shocked our conscience. We are still living in disbelief that it has happened.

Our only hope, let me say, is that the assistance that the United States and other members of the international community have been pouring in to help us, especially with technologies, will yield results. But the ability to push—and you have done that in this committee and beyond. We cannot rest until we find them.

Senator BOXER. So you would say that the country is shaken up about it, and that is across all areas of the country?

Ms. IBRAHIM. Mostly in the north.

And this also brings the discussion, which I put in the paper, about the difference between the north and the south. The incident of the Boko Haram and the Islamic fundamentalists are more in the north, and that is where we have sharia. In the south, we do not. So it is the ability not only to engage Nigerians but to engage Nigerians that are the sons and daughters of the soil, meaning people that work directly with some of the insurgencies and to see how we could long-term be able to slow down on this recruitment of—there is over 70 percent unemployed youth.

You are asking the question about what men can do. In our society, the women can hardly succeed without the men. And yesterday the Feminist Foundation and I were trying to call a figure, a sentence about what we thought about it. And we said something that it is this feeling of the patriarchal continuum syndrome that is still prevalent in some of our society. But I think this hearing will go beyond this room, and we hope we can run with it as we see also the passage of the CEDAW and the IVAWA.

Senator BOXER. Well, I hope the message goes out. Whoever is holding those girls, you are not living up to your manhood. Let those girls go.

So in my last question, I want to turn to the issue of this lack of enough, it seems to me, female peacekeepers around the globe. And I have long been working on that issue as well. According to your written testimony, only 3 percent of U.N. military and only 10 percent of U.N. police personnel are women. Now, we are the largest single contributor to the U.N. and the largest contributor to U.N. peacekeeping operations. What more can we do to help turn this around—it is absolutely wrong—to have more women in these positions?

Ms. O'NEILL. I agree. We can do a few things. As you mentioned, the United States is the largest financial contributor. We are not the largest troop contributor. So one of the areas of pushback that is often received at the U.N. is from national militaries and national police forces that we simply do not have the women in our forces to contribute. And if you want to go upstream on that problem and cut off that response, one of the things the United States can do is encourage more countries to create national action plans, so effective national action plans domestically that increase the recruitment and retention of women into national police and military forces. Right now, there are only about 43 countries in the world that have them, and many of the largest troop-contributing countries do not. Of course, you just cannot get more women into peacekeeping missions if they are not coming from these so-called feeder countries.

The second thing is we need to keep up the pressure on the Secretary General and on other member states to appoint more women to leadership positions across the United Nations. A couple weeks ago, we saw the first-ever appointment of a female military commander to lead the military portion of a U.N. mission. It was a big step and we need a lot more of those.

There has also been great pressure on the United Nations from countries like the United States in the last several years to appoint more women as heads of the mission, so again signaling and demonstrating that leadership role that the U.N. is able to walk the walk in terms of appointing women to be some of its senior leaders and demonstrate that to people around the world, men and women in their communities.

Finally, I would call attention to the issue of reviewing the mandates of peacekeeping and peace operations missions. So as a member of the Security Council, the United States has an opportunity to review the text that informs the purpose of those missions. And that is a prime opportunity to ensure that there is language inside there that calls for the members of those missions to consult regularly with women who are affected by conflict, to have more females in the troops and in the mission composition itself, and to make sure that the money that the United States and others are contributing are actually going to the priorities that this committee and others are identifying as essential not just for the effectiveness of the U.N. but for our broader global security.

Senator BOXER. Thank you very much.

I just want to say, because I need to run and vote now, this was a very important hearing, and I think the fact that we had everybody together in a way, even though it is not exactly the protocol, I think it is wonderful because I think when we listen to each other, the people who have the power to make the changes and the people who are on the ground in a nonprofit sense, it is a very important listening moment.

So what I hear everybody saying is we need to move on legislation that carries out this notion that is not very radical: that we are all created equally and we have to protect all segments of our population. I hope everyone within the sound of my voice—and there are people still outside. I am so sorry. We did not have any clue we would have such interest. We would have had a bigger room—should write to folks who are not yet on the International Violence Against Women Act and who have not yet declared in favor of ratification of CEDAW. Please write to those Senators. We are United States Senators. We represent the whole country. I think it is important that this country not stand with the most repressive forces in the world against CEDAW. It is ridiculous. It is embarrassing. It is inexplicable. And we need to get people in the Senate from both parties to help us with these two important movements, the CEDAW movement, the IVAWA movement, to put into law the fact that global women's issues need to be addressed because another administration could come in and say it is not important. So we need to get it into law. So if you could all help us with that.

And I just want to say to Ms. Ibrahim, thank you so much for your marvelous voice and to all of you.

And this notion that we are going to get, Dr. Barker, men to embrace this. I think we had a very iconic situation here when we had all those women Senators. You know, I would like to have a lot of male role models in the world sit here and say we have joined Dr. Barker in this notion that we are going to step out and say no to violence against women. And that would be an iconic photograph that I would love to arrange.

So to all of you who care so deeply about this, it means a lot to us up here because there are a thousand issues and you know what they are every day. They are all difficult and many are complicated. To me this is not complicated. This is an issue that has a solution. We have to make sure people understand every single person has to be respected and not violated. And it is a simple point. I do not think it takes that much energy to explain. But sadly there are some people who do not get it.

And so we need those role models. We need those voices. And I know so many of you in this room—I dare not start mentioning names because I would leave people out. Just keep up what you are doing and know that you have in this committee under the leadership of Senator Menendez and my subcommittee a place to come and a place to show the world that we care so much and to show this country that we care about our women and girls. As Senator Klobuchar said, we have issues in our own country, and we are going to tell other people what to do. We have got to make sure that our house is one that is clean.

So thank you for caring. As Barbara Mikulski often says, we will stand sentry on this issue. Thank you very much.

We stand adjourned. [Applause.]

And we will keep the record open for statements from other colleagues and questions.

[Whereupon, at 11:20 a.m., the hearing was adjourned.]

ADDITIONAL MATERIAL SUBMITTED FOR THE RECORD

RESPONSES OF AMBASSADOR CATHERINE M. RUSSELL TO QUESTIONS SUBMITTED BY SENATOR BY SENATOR ROBERT MENENDEZ

Question. South Sudan.—Gender-based violence—including rape, sexual assault, harassment, domestic violence, forced marriage, and survival sex—was a persistent problem in South Sudan prior to the current conflict. There is no doubt that with the current state of mass displacement, ubiquitous armed actors, the complete lack of rule of law, the situation has only deteriorated. Indeed, a recent UNMISS Human Rights report explains that all parties to the conflict have committed acts of sexual violence against women of different ethnic groups. UNFPA estimates that 24,500 South Sudanese women and girls are at risk of sexual violence.

Outside the U.N. bases, the dangers for displaced women and girls are the most severe. Women and girls face assault when they venture outside of the U.N. bases for livelihood activities and firewood collection. For example, one South Sudanese woman recently reported being raped three times in the last 2 weeks when collecting food for her family. While they are reluctant to leave the compounds and fear that they will be sexually assaulted by the armed actors outside, they take the risk because they understand that men would be killed if they leave, whereas women would "only" face sexual violence.

- ♦ What steps is the U.S. taking in cooperation with the U.N. to scale up com- prehensive GBV services, including medical and psychosocial support, both inside and outside of the U.N. bases?
- ♦ Will the U.S. provide funding to protection actors to set up safety patrols to accompany women on trips outside of the U.N. bases for firewood collection or livelihood activities, consistent with the Inter-Agency Standing Committee Guidance on Safe Access to Firewood and Alternative Energy in Humanitarian Settings?

Answer. So far in fiscal year 2014, the United States has provided more than $434 million to international and nongovernmental organizations to help conflict-affected people who have been displaced within South Sudan and forced to flee to neighboring countries. In addition to providing critical relief supplies and services, humanitarian actors, including those funded by the United States, are providing a multisector GBV prevention and response services, including access to specialized medical and psychosocial care for survivors, and material supports, both inside and outside of U.N. bases in South Sudan. In addition, all U.S. partners are required to ensure that the unique needs, safety, and dignity of women, girls, disabled, and other groups at increased risk of GBV, are factored into the design, delivery, and monitoring of assistance, ensuring that all U.S. funded programs include measures to promote the protection and well-being of the conflict affected populations.

U.S. partners are providing proactive, protective presence for at-risk individuals and communities facing specific threats or risks, and UNMISS is providing protective patrolling of access routes in and out of humanitarian response areas to deter violence against civilians. Partners are also using safety audits and safety assessments to monitor the changing environment and circumstances that can put women and girls at risk, promoting community-led strategies to mitigate risks and engaging the community in promoting gender-sensitive programming and services to meet the unique needs of the community. Ongoing protection monitoring efforts help partners ensure access to humanitarian services, identify risks, and adjust programs to reduce risks. Protection activities also support referrals for GBV survivors to provide appropriate survivor centered services.

The Inter-Agency Standing Committee Guidance on Safe Access to Firewood and Alternative Energy in Humanitarian Settings provides a valuable roadmap for humanitarian partners to identify the best household fuel strategy in both the acute and protracted phase of an emergency. During this acute phase and in light of the UNMISS mandate's increased emphasis on protection of civilians (POC), the United States is also encouraging UNMISS to conduct operations to secure key areas in towns to enable freedom of movement for IDPs. We are encouraging UNMISS to develop a system to inform IDPs and aid workers when a patrol is planned, so that IDPs can time their movements outside of the POC sites to coincide with these patrols.

In addition, our government is doing its utmost to help end this senseless conflict in the world's newest nation to enable the South Sudanese to direct their attention to eliminating the scourge of sexual and gender-based violence.

Question. The Global Summit to End Sexual Violence in Conflict.—We are pleased to see the U.S.'s leadership of the Call to Action on Protecting Girls and Women in Emergencies and the Safe from the Start initiative, both of which aim to address gender-based violence in conflict settings and other humanitarian crises.

♦   Following the recent global summit, are there additional concrete actions the U.S. plans to take that link the goals of the global summit with these ongoing initiatives?

Answer. The goals of the Call to Action on Protecting Girls and Women in Emergencies and the Safe from the Start initiative (which represents the U.S. Government commitment to the Call to Action) are closely aligned with the goals advanced by the June 9–13 Global Summit to End Sexual Violence. These efforts emphasize the need for comprehensive care for survivors of gender-based violence (GBV) in emergencies and the importance of practical steps the international community can take to help reduce the dangers that women and girls face in conflict and crisis situations around the world.

The United States worked closely with the United Kingdom to ensure that the Call to Action and the humanitarian dimensions of addressing sexual violence and other forms of gender-based violence were an integral part of the summit agenda and outcomes. In collaboration with UNICEF and UNFPA, the United States cohosted several expert-level sessions that addressed current efforts to strengthen the humanitarian system and build capacity within institutions to better prevent and respond to GBV from the start of an emergency. The sessions also provided field-based perspectives on needs, challenges and opportunities for survivor-centered prevention and response efforts in current emergencies, and on how we can scale up evidence-based approaches in humanitarian crises. These sessions were also an opportunity for the United States to urge other governments, U.N. agencies, and NGOs to sign on to the Call to Action communique and follow through on existing monetary and operational commitments to the Call to Action.

At the summit, the United States also provided an update on our efforts under Safe from the Start and our commitment to the Call to Action, including extensive stakeholder consultations to further develop and refine a roadmap for progress. Building on the success of the global summit, the United States will continue to identify and leverage all available opportunities for outreach at the global, regional, and local levels, to promote accountability and encourage concrete action and chance by key actors. In addition, the Department's Bureau of Population, Refugees, and Migration announced a new opportunity for nongovernmental organizations to compete for Safe from the Start funding to develop programs to prevent and respond to gender-based violence in acute refugee emergencies. Secretary Kerry also affirmed our intent to build on our initial $10 million commitment for Safe from the Start at the U.N. General Assembly this September, where we will launch several new programs and partnerships currently in development.

The Department of State and U.S. Agency for International Development look forward to building on the momentum generated by the summit to engage new stakeholders and continue to advance a strategic vision for collective action to tackle all forms of GBV. This will include strengthened coordination across all departments and agencies to implement the U.S. National Action Plan on Women, Peace and Security, and the U.S. Strategy to Prevent and Respond to Gender-based Violence Globally.

Question. Training for USG Personnel on Gender Integration.—In recent years, the USG has demonstrated that women and girls should be integral to all diplomatic efforts and has instituted mechanisms to ensure that all bureaus, both regional and functional, and missions in the field consider gender issues. Still, NGOs see a gap in training on gender issues for some field-deployed personnel that hinders robust programming on women's issues.

♦ Will the USG include mandatory training and capacity-building for all of our personnel on gender integration issues, particularly those deployed to regional hubs and bilateral missions?

♦ Training for field-deployed personnel should also include a full briefing on the U.S. National Action Plan on Women, Peace and Security, the U.S. Strategy to Prevent and Respond to GBV Globally, the Call to Action to End Violence Against Women in Emergencies, and Safe from the Start, to ensure that these initiatives are fully implemented at all levels.

Answer. The Department's Foreign Affairs Manual ("Promoting Gender Equality to Achieve our National Security and Foreign Policy Objectives"; 18 FAM 030) directs the Department to provide relevant training for our diplomats and development professionals on gender equality and advancing the status of women and girls in service of our national security and foreign policy objectives. In addition, Secretary Kerry has released policy guidance directing all Department bureaus and offices to further the implementation of 18 FAM 030, including expanding the structures, tools, and training necessary to institutionalize a focus on gender equality. As part of the implementation of these requirements, the Secretary's Office of Global Women's Issues (S/GWI) and the Foreign Service Institute (FSI) signed a Memorandum of Understanding in January 2013 to develop a stand-alone course on gender equality, with modules that could be included in other relevant regional, tradecraft, and leadership courses. The Department is exploring additional training initiatives and actions, including the possibility of mandatory training, to further build capacity of all employees on gender integration issues.

Since 2012, FSI's 3-day classroom course, "Promoting Gender Equality to Advance U.S. Foreign Policy Objectives," has trained more than 200 State Department personnel, including field-deployed employees. As part of the course curriculum, participants are required to read the U.S. National Action Plan on Women, Peace, and Security and the U.S. Strategy to Prevent and Respond to Gender-based Violence Globally. During the course, experts from the Department of State, USAID, and civil society engage course participants on how to implement these strategies, including in various regional contexts. FSI and S/GWI consult regularly with other Department bureaus and USAID to incorporate briefings on relative initiatives and opportunities, such as the Call to Action to End Violence Against Women in Emergencies, and Safe from the Start, into the course curriculum.

Additionally, FSI and S/GWI are developing an optional distance learning training course that will cover key definitions and the gender policy framework. This course, which will be accessible to all employees, will significantly further the Department's ability to train field-deployed employees on gender integration issues.

Question. Safe From the Start.—Last fall, Secretary Kerry announced the provision of $10 million for the Safe From the Start Initiative to prevent and respond to GBV in humanitarian emergencies.

♦ What specific programming has been developed to help women refugees?

♦ What specific positive actions and developments have resulted from the Safe From the Start funds?

Answer. The first organizations in 2013 to receive funding through Safe from the Start were the U.N. Refugee Agency (UNHCR) and the International Committee of the Red Cross (ICRC), two critical humanitarian organizations with global operations. ICRC is using the Safe from the Start funding to strengthen its global response to sexual violence, including in the Central African Republic and the Democratic Republic of the Congo, through programs including support for survivors and raising awareness in communities to reduce stigma and prevent further violence. UNHCR has developed a comprehensive program of action through Safe from the Start, including new mandatory training on GBV for all personnel, innovative new programs including a pilot financial empowerment initiative for Syrian refugee women in Cairo, Egypt facing GBV and community protection mechanisms in Uganda for South Sudanese refugees, and the creation of a new roster of emergency protection staff who will be responsible for strengthening the GBV response at the onset of a crisis. The first of these staff deployed to Erbil, Iraq, in May to assist arriving Syrian refugees, and additional personnel are preparing to start new assignments in Cameroon and Uganda to address the CAR and South Sudanese crises.

In addition, State/PRM is supporting the Women's Refugee Commission to develop a roadmap and consultative process around the Call to Action commitments. This will assist in bringing additional donors and stakeholders to the table to maximize our collective impact. State/PRM also released a new funding opportunity for non-governmental organizations on June 6, and proposals will be reviewed later this summer.

State and USAID are developing additional partnerships and programs and expect to announce these at the U.N. General Assembly in September.

————

RESPONSES OF SUSAN MARKHAM TO QUESTIONS
SUBMITTED BY SENATOR ROBERT MENENDEZ

Question. Haiti has been recognized by USAID as a country that is implementing gender-based violence (GBV) programming across all sectors. What are concrete examples of GBV programming implementation across the following sectors: Agriculture, Nutrition, Political Competition and Consensus Building, Public Health, Rule of Law and Human Rights, Education, and Civil Society Strengthening?

Answer. While USAID/Haiti is currently addressing GBV with programming across several sectors, the mission will expand to additional sectors as the post-earthquake reconstruction strategy is fully implemented. To ensure further GBV integration across the portfolio, USAID/Washington is sending a team of gender specialists to Haiti in August 2014 to review existing programs, suggest opportunities for GBV integration, and identify mechanisms for monitoring and evaluation. The team will also bring USAID staff working on GBV programming in different sectors together with local stakeholders and implementing partners.

GBV-RELATED PROGRAMING

USAID/Haiti addresses GBV both directly with targeted prevention, treatment and advocacy work and indirectly by empowering women through agriculture and economic growth programs that aim to elevate their status, improve their economic security, and reduce vulnerability to GBV.

PUBLIC HEALTH

Through the Haitian Group for the Study of Kaposi's Sarcoma and Opportunistic Infections (GHESKIO), USAID is providing female victims of sexual violence with access to integrated health services. Since 2012, over 3,000 GBV victims have been referred to voluntary counseling and testing for HIV services, reproductive health, and/or psychological support services. USAID is also training Haitian health care providers at 31 facilities on how to identify and manage GBV cases and provide referrals to social and legal services. Since 2012, more than 177,000 people have been sensitized and surveyed on GBV, including 485 staff, over 118,000 patients, and over 58,500 community members living in high-risk areas. The new service delivery program, awarded in September 2013, will expand treatment and support services for victims of GBV to additional health sites. USAID is also designing a new program, Combating Violence, which will aim to strengthen GBV survivor-centered services and referral pathways and prevent future GBV in emergency settings. It will focus on improving survivors' access to integrated services, including medical care and referral services, physiological care and support, and economic opportunities.

POLITICAL COMPETITION AND CONSENSUS BUILDING

During the coming election cycle, USAID will support efforts to comply with a recent constitutional amendment mandating a 30-percent quota of women in political parties and public life by training women candidates in communications and platform development, encouraging political parties to respect the 30 percent quota, and supporting civil society organizations to promote women candidates in the political process.

RULE OF LAW AND HUMAN RIGHTS

Haiti enacted legislation criminalizing human trafficking in 2014 with support from the U.S. Government. In collaboration with the Women's Parliamentary Caucus, USAID also plans to provide support on gender-based violence bills in the 2014 current legislative session. Through Collective Action for Security against Exploitation (acronym AKSE in Haitian Creole), USAID is strengthening advocacy efforts for human rights in the areas of gender-based rights, sexual and gender-based violence (GBV), and child protection.

EDUCATION

USAID is currently designing a program to increase equitable access to education, which leads to greater economic opportunity and reduced vulnerability to GBV. The program will target vulnerable populations, including street children and restaveks,[1] and address violence and GBV as barriers to access to education by providing psycho-social support to victims, training teachers and administrators in mitigation techniques, and raising awareness through classroom materials.

CIVIL SOCIETY STRENGTHENING

USAID provided support to three women's organizations, including the Commission of Women Victims for Victims (KOFAVIV), to establish a call center that provides public information on resources available to victims of GBV. Additionally, the human rights program referenced above, AKSE, will employ small grants to local institutions to provide services to victims and map existing informal SGBV and women's protective service networks, including providers specific to the lesbian, gay, bisexual, transgender, and intersex community.

AGRICULTURE

In addition to helping plant and harvest crops, women are the primary vendors at the marketplace, often referred to in Haitian Creole as "Madame Saras." Madame Saras benefit from USAID-supported investments in the value chain including access to credit, improved roads, and an SMS-based communication system providing market price information in real time. To date, USAID trained over 2,800 female farmers and certified 738 female master farmers in production techniques and natural resource management, helping to increase farm yields. Additionally, more than 40 percent of the nearly 13,000 farmers enrolled in the Haiti Hope mango program are women.

NUTRITION

The new Development Food Aid Program, awarded in August 2013, reduces food insecurity and vulnerability by supporting the Government of Haiti in establishing a safety net system and expanding capacities to prevent child undernutrition. The new program supports the Ministry of Women's Affairs and Rights with technical guidance on gender integration related to food security and social assistance programming. The program also supports activities to engage men in promoting female decisionmaking and participation and is piloting social and behavioral change communications strategies to challenge norms around masculinity and violence.

Question. The Global Summit to End Sexual Violence in Conflict.—We are pleased to see the U.S.'s leadership of the Call to Action on Protecting Girls and Women in Emergencies and the Safe from the Start initiative, both of which aim to address gender-based violence in conflict settings and other humanitarian crises.

◆ Following the recent global summit, are there additional concrete actions the U.S. plans to take that link the goals of the global summit with these ongoing initiatives?

Answer. The goals of the Call to Action on Protecting Girls and Women in Emergencies and the Safe from the Start initiative (which represents the U.S. Government commitment to the Call to Action) are closely aligned with the goals advanced by the June 9–13 Global Summit to End Sexual Violence. These efforts emphasize the need for comprehensive care for survivors of gender-based violence in emergencies and the importance of practical steps the international community can support to reduce the dangers that women and girls face in conflict and crisis situations around the world.

---

[1] A Haitian Creole term for children in forced domestic service.

The United States worked closely with the United Kingdom to ensure that the Call to Action and the humanitarian dimensions of addressing sexual violence and other forms of gender-based violence (GBV) were an integral part of the summit agenda and outcomes. In collaboration with UNICEF and the United Nations Population Fund (UNFPA), the United States cohosted several expert-level sessions that addressed current efforts to strengthen the humanitarian system and build capacity within institutions to better prevent and respond to GBV from the start of an emergency. The sessions provided field-based perspectives on needs, challenges, and opportunities for survivor-centered prevention and response efforts in current emergencies, and on how we can scale up evidence-based approaches in humanitarian crises. These sessions were also an opportunity for the United States to urge other governments, U.N. agencies, and NGOs to sign on to the Call to Action communique and follow through on existing monetary and operational commitments to the Call to Action.

At the summit, the United States provided an update on our efforts under Safe from the Start and our commitment to the Call to Action, including extensive stakeholder consultations to further develop and refine a roadmap for progress. Building on the success of the Global Summit to End Sexual Violence in Conflict, the United States will continue to identify and leverage all available opportunities for outreach at the global, regional, and local levels, to promote accountability and encourage concrete action and change by key actors. In addition, the U.S. Department of State's Bureau of Population, Refugees, and Migration (State/PRM) announced a new opportunity for nongovernmental organizations to compete for Safe from the Start funding. Secretary Kerry also affirmed our intent to build on our initial $10 million commitment for Safe from the Start at the U.N. General Assembly this September where we will launch several new programs and partnerships currently in development.

The United States looks forward to building on the momentum generated by the summit to engage new stakeholders and continue to advance a strategic vision for collective action to tackle all forms of GBV. This will include strengthened coordination across all departments and agencies to implement the U.S. National Action Plan on Women, Peace and Security, and the U.S. Strategy to Prevent and Respond to Gender Based Violence Globally.

Question. Safe From the Start.—Last fall, Secretary Kerry announced the provision of $10 million for the Safe From the Start Initiative to prevent and respond to GBV in humanitarian emergencies. What specific programming has been developed to help women refugees? What specific positive actions and developments have resulted from the Safe From the Start funds?

Answer. The first organizations in 2013 to receive funding through Safe from the Start were the Office of the U.N. High Commissioner for Refugees (UNHCR) and the International Committee of the Red Cross (ICRC), two critical humanitarian organizations with global operations. ICRC is using the Safe from the Start funding to strengthen its global response to sexual violence, including in the Central African Republic (CAR) and the Democratic Republic of the Congo, through programs including support for survivors and raising awareness in communities to reduce stigma and prevent further violence. UNHCR has developed a comprehensive program of action through Safe from the Start, including new mandatory training on GBV for all personnel; innovative new programs including a pilot financial empowerment initiative for Syrian refugee women in Cairo, Egypt, facing GBV; community protection mechanisms in Uganda for South Sudanese refugees; and the creation of a new roster of emergency protection staff who will be responsible for strengthening the GBV response at the onset of a crisis. The first of these staff deployed to Erbil, Iraq, in May to assist newly arriving Syrian refugees, and additional personnel are preparing to start new assignments in Cameroon and Uganda to address the CAR and South Sudanese crises.

In addition, State/PRM is supporting the Women's Refugee Commission to develop a roadmap and consultative process around the Call to Action commitments. This will assist in bringing additional donors and stakeholders to the table to maximize our collective impact. State/PRM also released a new funding opportunity for nongovernmental organizations on June 6, and proposals will be reviewed later this summer.

The Department of State and USAID are developing additional partnerships and programs and expect to announce these at the U.N. General Assembly in September 2014.

Question. Training for USG Personnel on Gender Integration.—In recent years, the USG has demonstrated that women and girls should be integral to all diplomatic efforts and has instituted mechanisms to ensure that all bureaus, both regional and functional, and missions in the field consider gender issues. Still, NGOs see a gap in training on gender issues for some field-deployed personnel that hinders robust programming on women's issues.

◆ Will the USG include mandatory training and capacity building for all of our personnel on gender integration issues, particularly those deployed to regional hubs and bilateral missions?

Answer. The USAID Gender Equality and Female Empowerment Policy requires all Agency staff who design, evaluate, or manage strategies and projects, or who directly or indirectly supervise these staff, to receive basic gender training. This includes live and online courses designed by the Office of Gender Equality and Female Empowerment (GenDev), colleagues in the Bureau of Policy, Planning and Learning (PPL) and USAID technical experts. In July 2012, GenDev hired a full time Training Coordinator who is responsible for the Agency's overall gender integration training strategy and designing courses with input from staff across the Agency.

ONLINE COURSES

"Gender 101: Gender Equality at USAID" is a mandatory online course to provide USAID staff with the basic knowledge and skills needed to ensure an understanding of, and a commitment to, gender equality and female empowerment in our Agency's work. The course also presents an overview of the goals and objectives of core gender-related policies and strategies guiding the Agency's work, including the Gender Equality and Female Empowerment Policy, U.S. National Action Plan on Women, Peace, and Security, and U.S. Strategy to Prevent and Respond to Gender-based Violence Globally. As of June 30, 2014, over 3,600 people, approximately one-third of all USAID staff completed this course.

"Gender 102: Putting ADS 205 into Action is a companion to Chapter 205 of USAID's Automated Directive System: Integrating Gender Equality and Female Empowerment in USAID's Program Cycle." Developed under the leadership of the Agency's Senior Gender Advisor in PPL and slated for release by the end of September 2014, this course will allow staff to develop skills to include attention to gender inequalities in country-level strategies, project designs, solicitations and evaluations. It also covers requirements and techniques for reporting on the USG standard Gender Equality and Female Empowerment indicators as well as on spending levels.

On June 30, 2014, the Office of Gender Equality and Female Empowerment launched "Gender 103: Gender 103: Roles and Responsibilities of Mission Gender Advisors," as an additional online resource for staff that includes strategies for carrying out gender integration in the Agency's everyday tasks, and tips on working with mission leadership and technical and program offices to integrate gender across all sectors.

LIVE COURSES

New Civil Service and Foreign Service employees learned about the importance of gender equality and integration during their orientations; as well as at a workshop for Foreign Service officers from around the world. A key component of the Agency's training strategy has been to offer gender trainings at regional hubs in Africa, Asia, the Middle East, Latin America and the Caribbean, and Europe and Eurasia, as well as customized gender training for bilateral missions to address their specific country contexts and specific challenges. These are coorganized by USAID's Regional Gender Advisors and the GenDev Office, with participation from technical staff with expertise in sectors such women, peace, and security; gender-based violence prevention and response; women's economic empowerment.

In addition, some bureaus and technical sectors have incorporated gender integration requirements or guidance into their live courses, or are doing so with the training currently under design. For example, gender has been well-integrated into Bureau for Food Safety and Global Health training courses, and in trainings for Global Climate Change. To support NAP implementation, specialized training opportunities focused on gender integration in crisis prevention, response, recovery, and transition environments were developed and are now part of USAID's regular complement of training (e.g., Gender and Conflict, Gender and Political Transition, Gender: Integration in Democracy, Human Rights, and Governance Programs). USAID has also implemented mandatory training requirements for disaster assistance response personnel designed to increase USAID's ability to deliver effective humanitarian assistance for women, men, boys, and girls. In fulfillment of the United States National Action Plan (NAP), all Office of U.S. Foreign Disaster Assistance (OFDA) staff are required to complete the Interagency Standing Committee (IASC) e-learning course, "Different Needs-Equal Opportunities: Increasing the Effectiveness of Humanitarian Action for Women, Girls, Boys, and Men." Additionally, all OFDA staff deployed on Disaster Assistance Response Teams in a program-related function are required to complete a training course on humanitarian protection.

Question. Training for field-deployed personnel should also include a full briefing on the U.S. National Action Plan on Women, Peace and Security, the U.S. Strategy to Prevent and Respond to GBV Globally, the Call to Action to End Violence Against Women in Emergencies, and Safe from the Start, to ensure that these initiatives are fully implemented at all levels.

Answer. All field staff with responsibility for programming receive basic information on key gender-related policies and strategies and how to implement them through Gender 101. This knowledge is supplemented with . . . GenDev trainings cover integrating gender-based violence prevention and response efforts into sectoral work. For example, the above-mentioned regional gender trainings in Africa, Asia. and the Latin America and Caribbean regions discuss how GBV issues (including trafficking) exist within sectors such as agriculture, energy, and infrastructure; how GBV impacts the LGBT community; how males can be both allies and victims; and what type of activities USAID could consider to address these issues. A recent series of gender integration training targeting field staff in missions in the Middle East and North Africa region, as well as live ''Operationalizing ADS 205'' courses have incorporated instruction on Women, Peace, and Security, including objectives and approaches for improving prospects for peace and security through the empowerment and protection of women and girls in conflict- and crisis-affected environments. USAID is also developing sector-specific toolkits that will help project design teams, project managers, and program officers integrate gender-based violence prevention and response efforts, as well as WPS objectives, into USAID programs. In addition, new Foreign Service officers are briefed on the U.S. Strategy to Prevent and Respond to Gender-based Violence Globally and National Action Plan on Women, Peace, and Security during orientation processes. This topic is also covered in the online Gender 101 training.

USAID will continue to provide resources and training to staff and to assist them with integrating gender issues effectively into their work and fulfilling the mandate of these key strategies and initiatives.

STATEMENT FOR THE RECORD SUBMITTED BY SENATOR MARIA CANTWELL (D. WA)

Thank you, Madam Chairwoman, for calling this hearing. Last year, I was proud to be an original co-sponsor for the reauthorization of the Violence Against Women Act, which protects American women against violence and human trafficking. I'm especially proud of the tribal provisions we included in VAWA, which are critical because nearly 40 percent of American Indian women will endure domestic violence in their lifetime, compared to 24 percent in the general population. VAWA ensures that violence prevention programs receive strong federal funding, and gives law enforcement powerful tools to fight violence and trafficking.

Violence against women is not just a problem in the United States; it's a challenge around the world. That's why I am proud to be a co-sponsor of the International Violence Against Women Act.

Madam Chairwoman, thank you for your leadership on empowering women around the world to stand up to violence. One key step to empowering women around the world is through access to education. Unfortunately, for many young women around the world today, educational opportunities are limited. According to the United Nations, only 35 percent of young women in Sub-Saharan Africa will receive a secondary education, let alone the college degree that opens up new opportunities for women in the workplace, and in leadership positions around the world.

But even though gender disparities in education remain high, especially in the developing world, countries and nongovernmental organizations are stepping up to the plate to make a difference. Today, I want to share the story of an organization which empowers young women in Rwanda by helping them receive a strong secondary-school education.

Rwanda was devastated by the war and genocide in 1994, but against all odds, Rwandans have managed to rebuild their country and become a model of low corruption, economic growth and gender parity in government. The constitution mandates a minimum 30 percent representation for women in parliament, and today, remarkably, it is 64 percent women. These women have been instrumental in the reconciliation and rebuilding of the country and continue to lead today. However, women are not represented at this level in all sectors, and in the rural areas, many parents are skeptical of the value of educating their girls. As is typical in many developing countries, if parents have limited money to send their children to school, many will send only their boys and keep the girls at home to help with household chores like collecting wood and tending to younger siblings. In Rwanda, 97 percent of girls attend primary school, but less than 13 percent attend secondary school, meaning that only a small fraction of Rwanda's young women will have the opportunity to go to university.

Rwanda Girls Initiative (RGI) was founded in 2008 in Seattle, Washington, with the mission of educating and empowering girls of Rwanda to reach their highest potential. RGI believes that education is the foundation on which all other development is built, and educating girls can exponentially increase this impact. With this belief, and with a strong partnership with the government of Rwanda, RGI started the Gashora Girls Academy of Science and Technology in 2011. Gashora Girls Academy is an upper-secondary university prep boarding school for 270 girls in grades 10–12 located in the Gashora sector of Bugesera District, a poor, agricultural area located an hour to the south of Kigali, the capital of Rwanda. This area was particularly devastated during the country's genocide in 1994. Gashora Girls Academy offers a curriculum that focuses on STEM subjects (science, technology, engineering, and math) with an underlying belief in the importance of educating and nurturing the "whole girl." Beyond the STEM coursework, students focus on developing life skills, leadership, critical thinking, and problem-solving abilities. Crucially, they get an education in a safe environment, free from the violence that is all too common for many young women in Rwanda and around the world.

In October 2013, Gashora Girls Academy graduated their first class of seniors. Of 85 graduates, 25 are admitted to schools in the U.S., including Harvard, Yale, Smith, the University of Pennsylvania, and Seattle University. Two more girls are going to McGill University in Canada. These 27 girls coming to North America will be receiving approximately $4.8 million in financial aid in order to attend worldclass institutions. Other graduating students are attending schools in Costa Rica, China, South Africa, Ghana, and right at home in Rwanda. These girls will become national leaders, doctors, scientists, teachers, and more, each contributing to the success of their country.

Enatha Ntirandekura is a recent graduate from Gashora Girls Academy. Both of her parents are subsistence farmers and the very little income they make is from a small plot of land. Though Enatha was always a strong student, some in her village discouraged her parents from allowing her to continue her studies. They said that a girl shouldn't be educated. At one point, someone in the village burned her family's coffee trees, their sole source of income. But her parents continued to send her to school, and she had the top score in her district on the national exam after middle school. She was offered a scholarship by the Rwanda Girls Initiative to attend Gashora Girls Academy. Enatha is a tenacious student and scored perfectly on the national exam she took after graduating this past year. Because of her success, she has been selected as a Presidential Scholar and will receive a full scholarship to an American university this fall. She hopes to study agriculture, and then go back to Rwanda to work on the problem of malnutrition and food scarcity to help her community.

As we can see from Enatha, educating a woman is a tremendous investment. When Enatha returns home with her degree in agricultural science, that one scholarship to Gashora Girls Academy will empower her to help many more people in Rwanda. And Enatha's story is not unique; in fact, it is the norm. One extra year of secondary school increases a girl's future wages by 15 to 25 percent. When a woman in the developing world receives seven or more years of education, she marries later and has fewer children. When women and girls earn income, they reinvest 90 percent of it into their families, creating a ripple effect for coming generations. Helping Enatha and the young women like her become doctors, teachers, and leaders will transform not only individuals, but entire communities.

Educating girls and young women is the surest way to empower them. Education empowers them to teach, to lead, and to stand up against violence. I am honored to stand with my female colleagues to draw attention to this important issue. A great education transforms lives and can lift up entire communities and countries. I look forward to working with the Chair and my colleagues to empower women and girls around the world.

––––––––––

STATEMENT SUBMITTED FOR THE RECORD BY SEN. SUSAN COLLINS (R. ME)

Madame Chairwoman, Ranking Member Paul, thank you for holding this hearing on a topic that could not be more timely. We are all aware of Boko Haram's kidnapping of nearly 300 schoolgirls in Nigeria in mid-April. They were targeted for the

52

sole offense of seeking an education. They are still missing, and the more time that passes, the more difficult it will be to reunite these girls with their families. And there are additional reports that Boko Haram kidnapped another 20 women a week ago.

Meanwhile, in India, two girls were found dead outside their village May 29; they had been raped and then hanged. Two more teenage girls were found hanged in India on June 12. In Pakistan last month, a woman was stoned to death by her own family members outside a court building in a major city, because her family was outraged that she married the man she loved rather than the man they had chosen for her.

These anecdotes illustrate a phenomenon that is well-documented. According to U.N. Women, the U.N. organization that promotes gender equality, 35 percent of women worldwide have experienced either physical or sexual abuse. In some countries, that figure rises as high as 70 percent. This type of violence ranges from domestic violence to rape and acid burnings to dowry deaths and so-called "honor killings." Violence against women and girls is a human rights violation, a public health epidemic, and a barrier to solving global challenges such as extreme poverty, HIV/AIDS, and conflict.

I believe the U.S. can and should be a leader in ending one of the biggest obstacles to not only U.S. national security but also global stability, development, prosperity, and human rights for all. This is why I am proud to be one of the original sponsors of the bipartisan International Violence Against Women Act (IVAWA, S. 2307), a bill that would ensure the U.S. has a comprehensive strategy in place to secure the safety and rights of women and girls, men and boys, across the world.

The International Violence Against Women Act—IVAWA—would ensure that the U.S. will continue to take a leadership role in combatting these problems. It would establish that it is the policy of the United States to take action to prevent and respond to violence against women and girls around the globe and to systematically integrate and coordinate efforts to address gender-based violence into U.S. foreign policy and foreign assistance programs. IVAWA would permanently authorize the State Department's Office of Global Women's Issues and the position of the Ambassador-at-Large for Global Women's Issues. It would require the Administration to develop and implement an annual strategy to prevent and respond to violence against women and girls for each of the five years after the date of enactment of this Act. This bill would ensure that efforts begun under President George W. Bush and President Obama to combat gender-based violence will continue in future Administrations.

Violence has a profound effect on the lives of women and girls. In addition to being a pressing human rights issue, such violence contributes to inequality and political instability, making it a security issue as well as a moral issue for us all. I am committed to continue working with my colleagues to end violence against women and girls and to provide the assistance and resources necessary to achieve this goal, and I call on all of my colleagues who are concerned about the global problem of violence against women and girls to join Senator Boxer and me in co-sponsoring the International Violence Against Women Act of 2014.

Madame Chairwomen, Ranking Member Paul, I thank you again for holding this hearing.

STATEMENT SUBMITTED FOR THE RECORD BY
CONGRESSWOMAN CAROLYN B. MALONEY (D. NY)

Chairman Boxer, Ranking Member Paul, I would like to thank you for hosting the hearing titled, "Combating Violence and Discrimination Against Women: A Global Call to Action" in the Senate Foreign Relations Subcommittee on International Operations and Organizations, Human Rights, Democracy, and Global Women's Issues.

I have long believed, like you, that it is critical we empower women on a global scale. It has been clear for many years that expanding opportunities for women not only improves their position in society, but also has a positive impact on economic growth and burgeoning democracies. It is of upmost importance that we continue to raise awareness and highlight the need for action on the fundamental right of equality for all.

That is why I introduced H. Res 19, expressing the sense of the House of Representatives that the Senate should ratify the Convention on the Elimination of All Forms of Discrimination Against Women (CEDAW). This bipartisan House Resolution urges the Senate to vote to ratify CEDAW, the landmark international agreement that mandates governments to take positive steps to ensure the full development and advancement of women, and their equal enjoyment of human rights, and that governments change or eradicate discriminatory laws, customs, and practices. Ratification of CEDAW would continue our nation's proud bipartisan tradition of promoting and protecting rights for all. Yet, the United States is the only western country in the world that has not ratified the treaty, although its fundamental principles of equality and nondiscrimination are central to our constitution. By not ratifying CEDAW, the United States becomes a bystander in creating a greater solution for women's equality around the world. The Senate's ratification of CEDAW would strengthen our standing as a global leader for the rights of women and girls everywhere.

I also reintroduced legislation in this Congress, HR. 2947, the International Women's Freedom Act, condemning violations of women's rights and gender equality while advocating for the improvement of the status of women around the world and the achievement of their equality with men. This bill would put in place a more sophisticated network for monitoring and evaluating the status of women worldwide. With a better evaluation system that includes greater consultation with both government groups and non-governmental organizations; more information on women's rights will be available to Congress and the public at large. This, vastly increases both the quality and quantity of information available to combat gross violations of women's rights. The bill also would require the U.S. Department of State to issue a report rating countries on their treatment of women. As is the case with the annual State Department Trafficking in Persons report, countries care about their ''score'' and work to improve their status, which ultimately helps the victims.

The United States needs high-level commitment in the form of laws which lay out explicit benchmarks for progress on women's rights around the world, backed by accountability mechanisms and the resources to achieve stated goals. Guaranteeing human rights for women is inextricably linked to a larger struggle for peace. development— and uniting for meaningful change. I strongly believe we owe it to the women of the world to shine a spotlight on the status of their rights in an effort to improve them.

STATEMENT SUBMITTED FOR THE RECORD BY ESTA SOLER, PRESIDENT AND FOUNDER, FUTURES WITHOUT VIOLENCE

On behalf of Futures Without Violence, I would like to thank the Members of the Senate Foreign Relations Subcommittee on International Operations and Organizations, Human Rights, and Democracy, and Global Women's Issues for holding this congressional hearing on one of the most compelling causes of our time: ending gender-based violence globally.

For more than 30 years, Futures Without Violence has led the way and set the pace for groundbreaking education programs, national and international policy development, professional training programs, and communication campaigns designed to end gender-based violence around the world. In 1994, FUTURES (then the Family Violence Prevention Fund) was instrumental in developing the landmark Violence Against Women Act passed by the U.S. Congress. Ten years later, FUTURES built a major coalition of experts from across the United States and around the world to tackle gender-based violence globally. Working together with congressional leaders in the House and Senate, we helped craft the International Violence Against Women Act (IVAWA) which the House and Senate both reintroduced in the 113th Congress with unprecedented bipartisan support.

This hearing comes at an opportune time. Advocates across the United States and local leaders around the world are applauding and calling for more U.S. government initiatives that provide a diplomatic, programmatic, and policy framework for the prevention and reduction of gender-based violence internationally. We applaud the U.S. government for presenting the first ever U.S. Strategy to Prevent and Respond to Gender-Based Violence Globally (Strategy) and U.S. National Action Plan on Women, Peace and Security (NAP). These two historic policy frames align closely with provisions in IVAWA. As a group, these form the foundation of efforts to achieve gender equality, promote women's and girls' empowerment, end gender-based violence, and institutionalize these approaches in U.S. foreign policy. In addition to the work undertaken by the U.S. government to implement the Strategy and NAP, FUTURES celebrated last year when the U.S. Congress reauthorized the Violence Against Women Act, which included important provisions to end child marriage internationally and also reauthorized the Trafficking Victims Protection Act.

The implementation of these initiatives arrives at a critical moment. Recent cases of horrific violence against girls and women in Nigeria, Pakistan, and India have galvanized the world around the need to address gender-based violence. Nations large and small, international agencies and financial institutions, nongovernmental organizations, and women and men of diverse communities, ethnicities, faiths, and political affiliations, all recognize that gender inequality and violence against women and girls are among the greatest barriers to global development, security, and prosperity.

Most importantly, this global movement is driven by the voices of those denied their most basic human rights simply because they are female. I am talking about the 23 year-old student gang-raped and beaten on a bus during her daily commute; the hundreds of girls abducted from school by militants and sold into forced marriages; the newly married 25 year-old bludgeoned to death by her father who disapproved of her choice in husband and sought to restore his family's honor; the teenage cousins raped and hanged while venturing to use a public restroom; the adolescent boys forcibly recruited to participate in violence; and the young girls whose breasts are "ironed" flat under the misguided notion that it will delay puberty and deter possible rape. Violence against women and girls and men and boys is an emergency every day and it claims a toll in every country.

All too often, the world's leaders are moved to act in the face of critically urgent and high profile emergencies, like the recent floods in the Balkans, the tragic aftermath of the earthquake in Haiti, and the typhoon in the Philippines. These crises demand urgent action—and it is imperative that such action takes into account the heightened vulnerability of women and girls to become targets of violence, sexual assault, and trafficking—but these leaders, and all of us, have to understand that violence is not relegated to times of great humanitarian crises and conflict—it happens every day.

In regions of armed conflicts horrific sexual and physical violence are being committed against women and girls and men and boys, often as a tool of war. The Democratic Republic of Congo remains ground zero for horrific acts of sexual violence, including sons being forced to rape their own mothers and young girls being kidnapped and gang raped on a regular basis.

Importantly, activists and leaders and everyday citizens around the world are taking action to stop the violence. I want to talk specifically about the role men can play in ending violence against women and girls. At Futures Without Violence, we began intentionally focusing on the role men can play in this work almost two decades ago. We asked men about their stake in the issue, and what they were willing to do to end the violence. We explored who helped them develop their attitudes and beliefs. Then we built on that research to create our Founding Fathers campaign through which, each Father's Day, men across the nation re-dedicate themselves to teaching the next generation that violence against women and girls is wrong. Founding Fathers include people like M.L. Carr, former all-star with your Boston Celtics; Ted Waitt, founder of Gateway Computer; Terry Lundgren, Chairman, President and CEO of Macy's; and hundreds of others.

Those lessons also led us to create Coaching Boys Into Men in 2002. It invites fathers, uncles, teachers, coaches and other men to teach the next generation that violence is always wrong. It has changed men's behavior in the United States, significantly increasing the number of fathers, and men, who talk to boys about violence. As a result, we adapted those strategies overseas. We are proud that, with support from our partners, we have put in place Coaching Boys Into Men in India, where cricket coaches and players are helping educate boys about the need to treat girls with respect. We have learned that when messages come from popular, respected coaches and players, boys listen.

Deep-seated change will only come when we stand together to stop this violence. There is a role for each of us.

With each passing day there is a growing understanding of the correlation between improving the status of women and girls and achieving peace and prosperity. Nations that promote gender equality and empower women and girls, and that remove the often formidable barriers for women and girls to access education, secure safe employment, participate in civic life, and live free from violence, also experience reductions in the rates of HIV and AIDS, decreases in incidents of child and maternal mortality, improvements in economic productivity, and the enrichment of participatory and democratic government. When we eliminate violence against women and girls and when we empower women and girls, everyone benefits.

The International Violence Against Women Act codifies many of the groundbreaking initiatives undertaken by the U.S. government that are having an immediate and direct impact in saving the lives of women and girls around the world. Most notably, IVAWA:

- Directs the Department of State and U.SID to continuing to implement a comprehensive multisectoral strategy to prevent and respond to gender-based violence;

- Integrates efforts to prevent and respond to violence against women and girls as part of U.S. foreign assistance programs including health, education, economic growth, legal reform, political participation, social norm change, humanitarian assistance, and foreign security training, among others;
- Supports overseas non-governmental and community-based organizations working to end gender-based violence; and,
- Ensures uniform data collection and accountability measures are in place to track investments in programs that address gender-based violence.

We need the U.S. Congress to stand together and affirm with unquestioned conviction that gender-based violence is not only deplorable, but is an issue that requires U.S. leadership. We need the U.S. Congress to move beyond the rhetoric and to pass the International Violence Against Women Act.

Ending gender-based violence is a moral imperative, but it is also an essential feature for building stable democracies, enabling economic development, and improving global security. This is an issue that rises above partisan politics. It is about the promotion of universal human rights and about creating a better world for everyone, women and girls, and men and boys alike. Thank you.

STATEMENT SUBMITTED FOR THE RECORD BY AMANDA KLASING,
WOMEN'S RIGHTS RESEARCHER, HUMAN RIGHTS WATCH

Chairwoman Barbara Boxer, Ranking Member Rand Paul, and other members of the Senate Foreign Relations Subcommittee on International Operations and Organizations, thank you for the opportunity to submit a written statement for today's hearing on violence and discrimination against women.

Human Rights Watch has been documenting violence against women as a human rights violation for almost a quarter of a century. We are pleased that your Committee is taking up this issue as a global call to action, as we believe that it will take significant leadership on the part of the United States to prevent, punish and eliminate violence against women globally, and to ensure adequate protections and services for survivors.

On June 13, 2014, Secretary of State John Kerry said in a statement at the Global Summit to End Sexual Violence in Conflict, held in London, "Gender-based violence, anywhere, is a threat to peace, security, and dignity everywhere." Human Rights Watch could not agree more. Gender-based violence is pervasive in the lives of hundreds of millions of women and girls around the world, including in our own country. It is well past time for Congress to take meaningful action to address violence against women globally, Violence against women spans geography, class, age, race, caste, creed, disability and sexual orientation, and eradicating it will require comprehensive understanding of its many manifestations. In this submission, Human Rights Watch would like to direct the subcommittee's attention to a few key areas of concern: child marriage; impact of conflict on women and girls; violence against women and girls with disabilities; and, women human rights defenders.

Child marriage

Child marriage occurs when at least one of the parties of a marriage is below 18 years of age. It is a violation of human rights that disproportionately affects hundreds of millions of girls and women. Child marriage also violates other human rights, including the rights to education, freedom from violence, reproductive rights, access to reproductive and sexual health care, employment, freedom of movement, and the right to consensual marriage.

Human Rights Watch has documented human rights violations against married girls in Afghanistan, Bangladesh, India, Iraq, Kenya, Malawi, Papua New Guinea, South Sudan and Yemen.[1] The accounts of the girls and women who were married as girls illustrate the profoundly detrimental impact of child marriage on their physical and mental well-being, education and ability to live free of violence. The consequences of child marriage do not end when child brides reach adulthood, but often follow them throughout their lives as they struggle with the health effects of being pregnant too young and too often, their lack of education and economic independence, domestic violence and marital rape.

The worst abuses linked to child marriage can be mitigated when governments set and enforce age limits for marriage, establish and enforce compulsory marriage registers, and prosecute perpetrators of forced marriage.

Impact of conflict on women and girls

Human Rights Watch first documented sexual violence in conflict in 1993 in a report about Indian security forces in Kashmir that used rape to brutalize women and punish their communities. Since then, we have investigated and documented rape in numerous conflicts around the world, most recently in Afghanistan, Central African Republic, Colombia, Democratic Republic of Congo, Cote D'Ivoire, Guinea, Libya, Somalia, Sri Lanka, and Syria.2 Regardless of the setting, we have found that efforts to hold attackers to account and medical and rehabilitation services for victims have largely been inadequate.

The international community has made progress in recognizing the prevalence of sexual violence and taken steps to address it. Rape in conflict is prosecuted as a war crime and a crime against humanity, and the United Nations Security Council, with leadership from the United States, passed a resolution in 2008 expressing its willingness to "adopt appropriate steps" to address widespread or systematic sexual violence. Security Council Resolution 1820 urges all parties to conflicts to provide sustainable assistance to victims of sexual violence in armed conflict and post-conflict situations. However, rape during and after war continues to terrorize women and girls, and impunity for these crimes is the norm. Most often survivors receive neither justice nor services, including comprehensive post-rape medical care.

In addition to sexual violence, Human Rights Watch has documented multiple abuses affecting women in war, including forced displacement; the targeting and punishment of women because of their own activism or activism by male relatives; the drive towards earlier, forced and child marriages because of instability and a lack of security for girls and younger women; an increase in domestic violence and sexual violence committed by civilians; lack of access to food, shelter and health care; the interruption of education; and, sexual exploitation and trafficking, to name but a few. When resources are mobilized to address sexual violence in conflict, they must also be deployed to address the full range of violations against women's and girls' rights that occur during and after conflict.

Lastly, women and girls may face specific and additional challenges to accessing education during conflict. In armed conflicts worldwide, students, teachers, and schools have been deliberately targeted. In some instances, female students and teachers and schools that educate girls and women are singled out. Armed groups have attacked, killed, and abducted female students because of opposition to girls and 4 women receiving an education, or in opposition to adolescent girls and women receiving an education alongside boys and men. In addition, since 2005, government armed forces and non-state armed groups have occupied and used schools and universities for military purposes in at least 23 countries with armed conflict. The use of schools for military purposes endangers students' and teachers' safety as well as their education. Girls studying alongside soldiers inside their schools may be sexually harassed, abused, and raped. Parents of girls are often particularly unwilling to send their girls to schools that are being occupied out of real or perceived concerns about such risks. Activities such as soldiers using school toilet facilities and excluding adolescent girls from using them also negatively affect girls' attendance and education.

Violence against women and girls with disabilities

Women and girls with disabilities who suffer gender-based violence face distinctive barriers to accessing gender-based and sexual violence prevention programs, post-violence medical care, and the justice system because of limitations in physical mobility, communication barriers, and isolation. These barriers leave them vulnerable to abuse, including physical and sexual violence.

In northern Uganda, for example, Human Rights Watch documented sexual violence against women with disabilities and found that more than one-third of 64 women with disabilities interviewed had experienced sexual or gender-based violence, often at the hands of relatives. Women with disabilities have a greater chance of being raped because abusers perceive them as less able to defend themselves or demand justice for violence. For women with disabilities, the process of reporting violence may be more difficult because of limited access, such as when limited mobility impedes their ability to reach justice institutions or when such institutions lack sign language interpreters. Several women with disabilities explained to Human Rights Watch how their efforts to seek justice for such crimes had failed. Because of the stigma already associated with disability and the stigma associated with rape, women with disabilities have enormous difficulty reporting incidents of sexual violence to the local authorities.

Women and girls with disabilities also face many challenges in accessing reproductive and sexual health services, which may only be exacerbated if they are a victim of gender-based violence. In many countries, women with disabilities face ignorance, discrimination and verbal abuse from healthcare personnel.

For example, our research in northern Uganda showed that women with disabilities who survive rape find it especially difficult to get post-exposure prophylaxis and other necessary treatment, such as emergency contraception, because of physically inaccessible transportation and healthcare facilities, as well as lack of confidentiality due to deaf women's need to bring family members as sign language interpreters.4

Emergency shelters for survivors of domestic violence are inaccessible to women with disabilities in many countries. In Turkey, Human Rights Watch researched the response to domestic violence in six cities, and found that none of these locations had domestic violence shelters (state or private) that could accommodate women with physical disabilities.

Women human rights defenders

In order to do our work effectively, Human Rights Watch collaborates closely with women and groups worldwide who fight for the rights of women. All human rights defenders may face risks, but we have seen firsthand that women defenders suffer additional threats and unique obstacles because they are women. The actions taken by governments are at times insufficient to address the gendered nature of risks and assaults. And even worse, we have documented examples where governments themselves target women human rights defenders.

Human Rights Watch has documented various abuses against women human rights defenders: physical attacks, hand-delivered threats, terrifying phone calls, sexual harassment, rape and threats against children of activists-all creating a chilling environment in an effort to silence these women. Often, no one is held accountable, and sufficient protection measures for these women are rare.

In some contexts, governments themselves target, arrest, and assault women because of their activism for women's rights. Human Rights Watch has documented sexual harassment and attacks on women by government forces for demonstrating in public. And, in some cases, women and girls have been arrested and abused by their male relatives because of their activism.

Many Human Rights Watch researchers have seen personally the tremendous toll that human rights work takes on women working at the grassroots level to seek justice for abused women, in particular victims of sexual violence. The women defenders I have worked with have been raped multiple times for their activism, have had their children threatened or abused, or have had to flee their homes. In one particularly difficult case, the stress of continuous threats led one woman defender to take her own life. I cannot imagine holding a hearing on the issue of combating violence against women without reflecting on the unmatched sacrifice and bravery of women human rights defenders around the world who are waging the difficult and daily fight to end violence in their own communities.

Recommendations

Human Rights Watch welcomes the global call to action raised by the Senate Foreign Relations Subcommittee on International Operations and Organizations, Human Rights, Democracy, and Global Women's Issues. Combatting violence against women requires a global effort to end abuses against women and girls. For years, Human Rights Watch has called for U.S. ratification of the Convention on the Elimination of All Violence against Women. We renew that call, and are disappointed that it appears unlikely that there are sufficient votes necessary for ratification. We will continue to ask for the ratification. However, as fundamental first steps, Human Rights Watch recommends that the U.S. Senate:

• Pass the bipartisan International Violence Against Women Act, S. 2307.
  • Request that the Secretary of State provide an update regarding the development and implementation of the multi-year and multi-sectoral strategy to end child marriage, as outlined in the domestic Violence Against Women Reauthorization Act passed in March 2013.
  • Press the administration to provide leadership at the U.N. Security Council for following up on its resolutions related to women, peace and security.
  • Call on the administration to provide public information regarding its progress in implementing the December 2011 U.S. National Action Plan on Women, Peace and Security and the U.S. Strategy to Prevent and Respond to Gender-Based Violence Globally, including lessons learned and best practices.
  • Ensure that U.S. funding for services to victims of violence includes comprehensive post-rape medical care.
• Urge the administration to show leadership in the global negotiations around the post-2015 sustainable development goals and push for the inclusion of a strong goal on gender equality and women's rights, including targets related to ending gender-based violence, ending child marriage, and ending all forms of discrimination against women, all with clear target dates.

- Strengthen the U.S. commitment to addressing accountability and justice for sexual violence in conflict by developing relevant benchmarks for all U.S. assistance related to security sector reform, such as visible and clearly defined efforts from the recipient government to investigate and prosecute serious violations of international humanitarian law. This entails prosecuting individuals who were criminally liable because they ordered such crimes or who as a matter of command responsibility failed to prevent or punish them.

STATEMENT SUBMITTED FOR THE RECORD BY DR. NANCY OKAIL, EXECUTIVE DIRECTOR, TAHRIR INSTITUTE FOR MIDDLE EAST POLICY

To the Honorable Chairwoman Barbara Boxer, Ranking Member Rand Paul, and Members of the Subcommittee:

Thank you for convening this important hearing to examine the growing threats to safety and security of women around the world. The Tahrir Institute for Middle East Policy is very grateful, Madam Chairwoman, for your many efforts to strengthen protections for women globally through engagement with both U.S. officials and our international partners at the United Nations and around the world. It is an honor to submit my testimony before the first congressional subcommittee specifically charged with addressing global women's issues.

Efforts to address gender inequality over the last several decades have resulted in considerable advancements in women's rights. In that time, the international community has embraced increased international legal protections for women and girls, including, notably, the U.N. Convention on the Elimination of All Forms of Discrimination against Women, which has been ratified or acceded to by nearly every U.N. member state (although, regrettably, not the United States). Additionally, the constitutions of more than 130 countries now guarantee gender equality, and more than 115 countries outlaw sexual harassment and gender violence.

Despite these important advances, as the United Nations said nearly 20 years ago, "no society treats its women as well as its men." Unfortunately, that remains as true today as it was then. Much more work remains to be done to combat violence and discrimination against women around the world, particularly in the Middle East. As we have seen in Egypt, women continue to be subordinated by a society that embraces patriarchal social norms and diminishes or ignores the daily sexual harassment and increasingly frequent mass sexual violence perpetrated against women. The failure by the government of Egypt to adequately enforce its domestic and international legal obligations to protect women has contributed to a culture of impunity that severely undermines efforts to achieve gender parity in Egypt.

I am grateful for the opportunity, Madam Chairwoman, to join your global call to action to address these problems, and hope that the following assessments and recommendations will be valuable in reversing this very disturbing trend.

Discrimination and violence against women and girls in Egypt

Gender inequality

The problem of gender inequality in Egypt is one that affects all aspects of daily social, political, and economic life for women. According to the World Economic Forum's 2013 Gender Gap Index, which measures the gap between men and women across four categories, Egypt ranks 125 overall out of 136 countries, putting only a few paces ahead of Syria, Saudi Arabia, Iran, and Yemen. These rankings factor into account women's economic participation and opportunity, educational attainment, health and survival, and political empowerment. Comparatively, the Middle East ranks last among other regions in closing the gender gap. The region has only closed 59 percent of the gender gap between men and women (by comparison, North America has closed 74 percent of its gender gap).

The wide gender gap between men and women in Egypt is largely attributable to social norms: Egyptian society is in many ways patriarchal, and the family is considered to be the main unit of society. As a result, women's primary role in society is widely viewed to serve a caretaker function, although many women are informally employed. Men, meanwhile, are regarded as the breadwinner and head of the family.

Unfortunately, this social perception of a woman's place in society was recently echoed in remarks made by then-candidate Abdel Fattah al-Sisi, who called upon to women to "encourage [their] husbands and children to work," reflecting the deeply-ingrained view that a woman's proper place is at home. Sisi went on to say that women should help to save electricity by "going around the house and turning off the lights," and referred to women as the "calm, soft, and rational voice in the house"—in both instances overtly suggesting that women belong at home, rather than in the workforce.

This social structure may explain why the literacy rate for women remains far below that of men. The 2013 Gender Gap Index reports that the female literacy rate in Egypt only stands at 66 percent, compared with 82 percent for males. According to one woman, "reading doesn't make a woman socially acceptable or useful." Indeed, while education rates for girls and boys are reported to be virtually the same for primary and tertiary education levels, in many rural areas—where girls are sometimes not even registered with the state after being born—an estimated 80 percent of girls do not attend school.

Low literacy rates and social expectations of women keep them from becoming contributing members of the labor market. According to the 2013 Gender Gap Index, women's labor force participation in Egypt only stands at 25 percent, compared with 78 percent for men. These rates remain largely unchanged from 2011, when, according to the U.N. Children's Fund (UNICEF), only 22 percent of Egyptian women aged 15 and above were actively engaged in the labor market by either working or looking for work, compared with 75 percent of Egyptian men. By comparison, the global labor participation rate for women was 52 percent in 2011.

Women's low labor force participation helps to perpetuate the social expectation that women will stay at home, which may in turn help to explain why women's political empowerment in Egypt is also low as compared with international rates. The 2013 Gender Gap Index found that only 12 percent of Egypt's ministers and 2 percent of its parliamentarians are female. Globally, women make up more than 20 percent of national parliaments, nearly 6 percent of the world's heads of state, and close to 8 percent of heads of government, putting Egypt behind the international average.

We have seen some recent efforts to improve women's political participation in Egypt. An earlier-proposed version of Egypt's parliamentary elections law would have required that 24 seats in Egypt's new parliament (4 percent of the 603 total number of seats) be set aside for women. A recently-revised law now sets aside 40 seats for women, or 6 percent. While these rates would mark an improvement in women's parliamentary representation over last year's 2 percent rate, they still fall far below the international average, and of course do not reflect the fact that women make up nearly half of Egypt's population. By keeping women out of politics in Egypt, they are denied opportunities to strengthen legal protections and participate in decision-making structures that could help to elevate the status of women and girls.

Female genital mutilation

Discrimination and violence against women in Egypt is a problem that often begins during girlhood. Patriarchal social stigmas surrounding women and their role in society have resulted in their being cast as symbolic representatives of the family's "honor." As a result, the violation of a woman's sexual purity—be it through rape, assault, sexual promiscuity, or some other offense—is considered a violation of a family's honor.

In order to reduce a woman's sexual desire and maintain her purity and faithfulness, the parents of young girls often subject their daughters to female genital mutilation (FGM), which involves the circumcision of a girl's clitoris. Indeed, the practice has no effect on sexual desire, but instead makes sex painful for women. According to UNCEF, 91 percent of women in Egypt between the ages of 15 and 49 have been subjected to FGM. The practice confers absolutely no medical benefit, and is instead a violation of a child's right to health, security, physical dignity, and right to be free from torture or cruel, inhuman, or degrading treatment, as well as the right to life (where cases result in death).

The crime has been outlawed since 2008 but the FGM ban has never been enforced in the courts until now, after one young girl died last year following a botched FGM procedure. The incident has led to the country's first prosecution of the crime. The crime is punishable by a prison term of anywhere from three months to two years, and a fine of up to EGP 5,000 (U.S. $700).

Sexual harassment and violence

The problem of sexual harassment and violence against women are, regrettably, common occurrences in Egypt, and have been for years. According to a 2013 study released by the United Nations Entity for Gender Equality and the Empowerment of Women (U.N. Women report), 99.3 percent of Egyptian women have experienced some form of sexual harassment, ranging from verbal remarks to physical touching. The majority of women interviewed for the study said that harassment occurs regardless of attire, looks, age, marital status, or economic class. Likewise, violence against women in Egypt is an endemic problem that led to Egypt being labeled the "worst Arab state for women" last year. (Other factors surveyed included women's status within the family, reproductive rights, and women's political and economic participation.

Unfortunately, since the start of Egypt's revolution three years ago, reports of harassment and violence against women has gone up as more and more women occupy public spaces.

According to several Egyptian non-governmental organizations, more than 500 sexual violence survivors experienced assaults between February 2011 and January 2014. A separate group—Shoft Taharosh ("I Saw Harassment")—reportedly documented 730 cases of sexual harassment in October 2012, only three of which were reported to the police.

Several of the more violent attacks against women have gained worldwide attention. The international community reacted with outrage, for instance, to the violent mob assault in February 2011 against CBS reporter Lara Logan, who was covering protests that led to the downfall of former President Hosni Mubarak, and to reports last July that more than 150 counts of sexual mob attacks had occurred in Tahrir Square during protests that led to the ouster of former President Mohamed Morsi.

The international community was shocked once again when, two weeks ago, violent mobs sexually assaulted several women in Tahrir Square during celebrations of Mr. Abdel Fattah al-Sisi's presidential election. The imagery of dozens of men sexually assaulting a lone woman in a video of one of the attacks incited strong emotional reactions among Egyptians as well, which ranged from summary condemnation of the incident to a dismissal of the attack as the product of excessive "celebration." Blame was ascribed to the Muslim Brotherhood, accused of committing the violence in an attempt to ruin Sisi's celebration, as well as to the victims themselves.

In his response to the incident, even President Sisi failed to adequately address the cause of such violence. In a public apology to the victim, whom President Sisi visited in the hospital—along with a spray of television cameras to capture the moment—he remarked that "our honor is being violated on the streets." Overlooked in his remarks is the fact that it is not Egypt's honor that is being violated, but women's bodies and sense of human dignity.

President Sisi's public acknowledgement of this problem is laudable, but his choice of words is regrettable, because it is precisely this concept of "honor" that often discourages victims from reporting abuses them. A woman may be urged by her family or the police to keep quiet about the incident in order to avoid bringing shame upon the family or upon the victim—as if the victim was somehow complicit in her own attack.

Indeed, the notion of personal or family honor is one of the reasons that women do not report abuses committed against them. According to the U.N. Women report, nearly 35 percent of women surveyed claimed that they did not report incidents of harassment to the police either because they feared for their reputation or for their family's reaction. Both this notion of honor and the problem of victim-blaming are deeply entrenched in Egyptian culture. Often, female victims will be blamed for provoking the attacks because of the clothing or makeup they wear. This harmful discourse places the blame for such attacks on the victim, releasing the perpetrators from culpability.

In the same report, another 23 percent of women said that they failed to report the incident because they did not know that harassment was illegal. It is incredible to think that the harassment of women in Egypt is so common, systematic, and undisciplined that nearly a quarter of Egyptian women do not even know that it is a crime and that they have a right to be free from such abuse.

Also telling of the problems intrinsic in Egypt's legal and judicial system is the fact that almost 10 percent of women in the survey said that they feared they would be harassed by the police if they tried to report the abuse. Those fears are not unfounded: among women who had reported harassment, 5 percent said that they were harassed by police when they tried to file a complaint, while nearly 14 percent said that the police scolded and mocked them.

The state's complicity in perpetuating this violence goes beyond simply discouraging women from filing complaints: security and police forces also perpetrate sexual violence against women, with impunity. In early 2011, allegations surfaced that the military had conducted so-called "virginity tests" against female detainees. According to remarks made by then-General al-Sisi, who defended the tests, the military needed to determine whether the women were virgins in order to protect the military from rape allegations—insidiously implying that only virgins can be raped. Of course, abuses by the military and police forces against women did not end there. Continued abuses produced protests against law enforcement officers in late 2011 and mid-2012, further confirming the perception that reporting such crimes to institutions that abet them is a lost cause.

Assessment of recent commitments by the government of Egypt to address violence

Legal reforms

Until recently, the crime of sexual harassment was not specifically defined under Egyptian law. That changed on June 5, 2014, when, just days before leaving office, former interim President Adly Mansour issued Decree No. 50 of 2014 which amends Egypt's penal code to define the crimes of harassment and sexual harassment, and imposes increased penalties for certain violations.

According to the amendments, harassment is now defined as when one "approaches another person in a public, private, or familiar place with sexual or suggestive objects, suggestions, or insinuations, be it by allusion, word, or action in any way, including wired and wireless communication networks." Harassment is punishable by a term of imprisonment of not less than six months or a fine of EGP 3,000 (about U.S. $419). Repeat offenders may be punished by a prison term of one year and the fine to EGP 5,000–10,000 (about U.S. $700–1,400).

The behavior defined above is considered sexual harassment if done "with the purpose of the criminal receiving benefit of a sexual nature from the victim." The crime is punishable by a minimum prison term of one year and a fine of EGP 10,000–20,000 (about U.S. $1,400–2,800). Any individual who is in a position of authority over the victim "through employment, family or education," or if "the crime was committed by two or more people, or at least one of the offenders is armed with a weapon," will be punished with a term of imprisonment of between two and five years and a fine of EGP 20,000–50,000.

The penal code defines rape as "sexual intercourse with a female without her consent." The penalty for rape is life in prison, but in cases where the victim is a minor or the rapist has a position of employment, familial, or educational authority over the victim, the penalty can include capital punishment.

National strategy

Last week, newly-elected President Sisi proposed additional measures to combat the problem of sexual violence in response to the violent sexual assaults against women in Tahrir Square. Among other things, President Sisi ordered the formation of a ministerial committee that included representatives from the government, Muslim and Christian religious establishments, and civil society to identify "the underlying causes behind the proliferation of this phenomenon and delineate a national strategy to address it."

On June 12, the committee announced its plan to tackle sexual harassment, which includes an increase in security presence in public squares; the creation of an "integrated security team" to combat sexual harassment and assault; an increase in police officers assigned to the interior ministry's human rights sector to respond to sexual harassment and assault claims; implementing Egypt's newly-amended sexual harassment provisions; researching the causes of such abuse to create a national strategy to combat it; amending school curricula to include lessons on equality and violence against women; and launching public education campaign during Ramadan. The plan also includes asking state hospitals to care for victims of sexual assaults (incredibly, one of the victims of the recent Tahrir Square assaults was turned away from several public hospitals before being admitted to a private one).

Assessment

Many of these proposals by the government of Egypt to tackle the problem of sexual assault against women are laudable, and could mark the turning page for Egypt—if the government follows through on its commitments. At the same time, some of these proposals do not go far enough in addressing the problem and need to be reconsidered.

The recent amendments to Egypt's penal code are a step in the right direction, but certain provisions still make it difficult to prosecute sexual harassment. For instance, the crime of sexual harassment requires the perpetrator to have intended to receive sexual gratification from the victim. A defendant need only claim that his actions were accidental or not intended to be harmful, and the burden of proof thus shifts to the prosecutor—and thereby, the victim—to prove the defendant's culpability.

Rather than making it all but impossible for victims to prove that they were harmed, the focus of the law in punishing sexual harassment should instead be on the abuse committed and its effect on the victim, rather than the intent of the perpetrator. The government should re-amend this provision to eliminate the burdensome intent requirement.

Other provisions of the penal code also place an inordinate burden upon the victim in proving her victimization. The amendments to the penal code, for example, did not eliminate the existing requirement that a victim of sexual harassment bring her harasser and two witnesses to the police station in order to file a claim. This provision effectively perpetuates patriarchal norms by suggesting that the victim's word is not good enough to be taken at face value.

The law should be amended to eliminate the requirement that the victim furnish the perpetrator and witnesses. The responsibility of procuring witness statements and interviewing the accused should rightly fall upon the police, who are charged with enforcing the law. Police, for their part, should be trained and equipped to properly investigate allegations of sexual harassment and violence.

Also problematic in the penal code is the definition of rape, which only criminalizes "sexual intercourse with a female without her consent." The law fails to account for rape by other means, including anal and oral penetration, and also only criminalizes intercourse, which does not include penetration by other body parts or instruments. Unfortunately, many victims of gang rapes have been assaulted with sharp objects and fingers, which are not covered under the rape law. Moreover, the law only considers women to be the plausible victims of rape, completely excluding male victims, many of whom are victimized by police forces in prison.

The penal code should be amended to more broadly define rape as the vaginal, anal, or oral penetration of a male or female by intercourse, other body parts, or instruments, without consent or in coercive circumstances that negate consent.

The enactment of improved laws is an important first step in trying to tackle the sexual harassment epidemic facing Egypt, but the law is only a useful tool in combating these crimes if it is properly enforced, and there we see additional problems. Police are sometimes complicit in attacks against women, and often lack the training and capacity to properly process such complaints.

While an increased security presence in public squares may, theoretically, help to deter sexual violence against women, police are also part of the problem. According to the U.N. Women report, 17 percent of reported cases of sexual harassment are perpetrated by police and security officers. Without a commitment by the government to hold officers accountable for abuse, an increased police presence may only exacerbate the problem.

The government must fully acknowledge that the extent of this problem goes beyond private actors and includes the government itself. Egypt must dedicate itself to holding its own officials accountable for violating the same laws they are responsible for enforcing.

Police are not the only perpetrators of sexual abuse who escape with impunity. Lax law enforcement procedures and corrupt police practices have led to deeply troubling trends in the miscarriage of justice, as reflected by the many accounts of arbitrary arrests and forced disappearances in Egypt. It is not uncommon for innocent individuals to be charged with crimes that they did not commit, either because the prosecutions are pursued as a form of retribution against the defendant or his family, or because police are pressured to close out cases. In the latter instance, police often arbitrarily arrest young men, typically from poorer neighborhoods, who are less likely to have the resources or connections to avoid arbitrary arrest or detention.

This form of miscarriage of justice has led some to question whether the newly-amended sexual harassment laws will be appropriately enforced, or whether enforcement will only be selectively directed at certain individuals. It is not an absurd notion to consider, given that the government has also attempted to silence its critics by routinely targeting opposition leaders, activists, NGO workers, and journalists for malicious prosecutions based on fabricated charges.

While we applaud plans by the government to increase security sector resources to respond to sexual crimes, given the prevalence of lax investigatory and enforcement procedures, the government must ensure that all police officers are properly equipped to address sexual abuse claims and are properly trained in due process standards in order to avoid miscarriages of justice.

Other measures recently announced by the government to address this issue include researching the causes of sexual abuse to create a national strategy to combat it; amending school curricula to include lessons on equality and violence against women; and launching a public education campaign on sexual harassment.

All of these proposals are commendable, but to be successful and have buy-in from relevant stakeholders, their implementation must include input from civil society actors, including women's and human rights groups, victim treatment centers, survivors' groups, educators, religious leaders, and other important actors.

Moreover, although we likely will not know the details of the national strategy for several weeks or longer, any plan proposed by the government should adopt measures that ensure adequate medical and psychological support for victims of sexual assault. These measures should address victim confidentiality, the provision of timely treatment, support for rehabilitation and recovery, referrals to other services. Police and medical officials should receive training on these measures.

Recommendations for the U.S. Government

While the Egyptian government has taken commendable steps in addressing the issue through the recent ratification of a new law criminalizing sexual harassment, there is much left to accomplish. As a strategic ally to Egypt, the United States government can play an important role in encouraging Egyptian leaders to take appropriate measures, as described above, to meaningfully address systemic discrimination and violence against women. The U.S. government can also ensure that adequate funding is provided for programs that advance these goals.

- Engage with Egyptian government leaders and encourage them to adopt the measures outlined above to ensure that Egypt's legal protections and social norms more fully protect the rights of women and girls;
- Ensure that U.S. funding to Egypt supports programs that will strengthen Egypt's public education and awareness-raising efforts on the topics of equality and violence against women, and also support public education programs and campaigns on the topic of female genital mutilation;
- Continue to provide funding that supports women's and girls' education, and work with Egyptian leaders to ensure that all girls—particularly those living in rural areas—are properly registered so that they can receive an education;
- Continue to support civil society groups in Egypt that are working to address the problems of discrimination and violence against women, and encourage the government of Egypt to engage and collaborate more directly with civil society leaders on these issues; and
- Encourage Egyptian leaders to consider revising the parliamentary elections law to allow for greater female representation in Egypt's parliament, and support U.S. aid programs that empower women to become more politically engaged.

STATEMENT SUBMITTED FOR THE RECORD BY AMNESTY INTERNATIONAL

Thank you Chair Boxer, Senator Paul, and to the members of the Committee, for holding this important hearing and for your leadership in helping to end gender based violence globally.

Amnesty International U.S is pleased to testify at this critical and timely hearing. Amnesty International's testimony will focus on the international human rights framework that exists to address gender-based violence, and offer recommendations on concrete actions that the United States Government can take to help prevent, respond, and ultimately end the violence.

Our organization's campaigns to end gender-based violence around the world have produced hundreds of reports documenting these human rights abuses; offered detailed recommendations for action by governments, non-state actors, and international organizations; and clearly illustrated the connection between this violence and other violations of human rights around the world.

Violence against women takes many forms, including rape, domestic violence, female genital mutilation, child and forced marriage, and acid attacks to name a few. It's a global human rights crisis that exacerbates instability and insecurity around the world.

But is also an issue that affects individual women intimately. United Nations statistics show that one in three women will be raped, beaten, coerced into sex or otherwise abused during their lifetime. A shocking number and potentially a vast underestimation of the true number of women affected.

Over the last 25 years, violence against women has increasingly been understood and accepted as a human rights issue. Whereas violence was previously dismissed as an unpreventable consequence of war, cultural norm, or simply a private matter, the international community has acknowledged that women and girls often are targets of abuse because of their gender—whether in conflict, where rape is often used as a weapon of war, in communities and schools, or in the home where violence occurs within the family. These crimes are now recognized as human rights abuses that governments must prevent, prohibit and punish.

Amnesty International has recommended four U.S. policy initiatives which will make a significant impact in the work to end gender-based violence globally. These are:

- Passage of the International Violence Against Women Act;
- Passage of the Women, Peace and Security Act;
- U.S. promotion of reform of laws and policies that discriminate against women and girls, and;
- U.S. ratification of the Women's Treaty, officially known as the Convention on the Elimination of All Forms of Discrimination Against Women (CEDAW).

We see progress on two of our past recommendations to Congress—the promulgation of both a U.S. Strategy to Prevent and Respond to Gender-Based Violence Globally and a U.S. National Action Plan on Women, Peace and Security. But much work remains to be done.

Every day, women and girls around the world are threatened, beaten, raped, mutilated, and killed with impunity. Worldwide, nearly one billion women will be beaten, coerced into sex, or otherwise abused in her lifetime, whether at the hands of family members, government security forces, or armed groups.

Today, what unites women internationally—transcending class, race, culture, religion, nationality and ethnic origin—are violations of their fundamental human rights, and their persistent efforts to claim those rights.

Human rights framework

The rights of all women as human beings, around the world, were first and most fundamentally recognized by the Universal Declaration of Human Rights (UDHR). Adopted in 1948 by the U.N. General Assembly, the UDHR states in clear and simple terms rights that belong equally to all people in all nations, "without distinction of any kind such as race, color, sex, language . . . or any other status."

The Convention on the Elimination of All Forms of Discrimination Against Women is the first and only international treaty to comprehensively address women's rights within political, cultural, economic, social and family spheres. Adopted by the U.N. in 1979, CEDAW provides an international standard for protecting and promoting women's human rights and is often referred to as a "Bill of Rights" for women.

The 1993 U.N. Declaration on the Elimination of Violence Against Women (DEVAW) sets forth ways in which governments should act to prevent violence, and to protect and defend women's rights. DEVAW calls on states to "exercise due diligence to prevent, investigate and, in accordance with national legislation, punish acts of violence against women, whether those acts are perpetrated by the state or by private persons."

The Geneva Conventions designate many acts of sexual violence—including rape, enforced prostitution, sexual slavery, and sexual mutilation—as war crimes, and grave breaches of the Conventions.

The U.N. Protocol to Prevent, Suppress and Punish Trafficking in Persons, Especially Women and Children defines human trafficking as the illegal recruitment, sale, transport, receiving of, and/or harboring of human beings through force, deceit, coercion or abduction for the purpose of all forms of forced labor and servitude (Article 3(a)). Many cases of sexual violence during armed conflicts occur under conditions of slavery.

The Rome Statute of the International Criminal Court is the first international treaty to expressly recognize a broad spectrum of sexual and gender-based violence as constituting genocide, war crimes and crimes against humanity, and is the first time that sexual slavery and trafficking have been expressly recognized as crimes against humanity in an international treaty. The majority of cases that have been brought before the ICC to date involve gender-based violence.

U.N. Security Council Resolution 1325 and subsequent related resolutions emphasize the responsibility of all states to put an end to impunity and to prosecute those responsible for war crimes involving sexual and other violence against women. It calls for an increase in the participation of women at decisionmaking levels in conflict resolution and peace processes. It also calls for the protection of human rights of women and girls during the reconstruction process, particularly as they relate to the constitution, the electoral system, the police, and the judiciary. Six subsequent resolutions have been passed since 1325 that further aim to protect women and girls from conflict-related sexual violence and promote their role in the peacemaking process.

Violations of women's human rights

The ways in which women experience human rights abuses are unique. While human rights are understood as the rights that everyone has by virtue of their humanity, the assumption that all humans have the same experiences and needs is particularly problematic for women.

Historically, states have assumed responsibility for human rights violations only when state agents or officials were the perpetrators, and certain forms of violence against women by state agents have been acknowledged as torture. However, women more often face abuses from non-state actors, such as their employers, partners, husbands, families, friends and community members. It is critical to note that whether abuses against women are committed by state or non-state actors, in the public or private spheres, the state is obliged to condemn, prevent and punish all acts of violence against women and to take measures to empower women.

When international law is applied without an understanding of the state's responsibility for abuses committed by private actors, women are denied an essential part of the protection that the human rights system is supposed to provide. When the state dismisses the majority of violence against women as private or domestic matters, thereby allowing this violence to continue, it sends a clear message that violence against women is condoned.

Human rights abuses against women are often complicated by further discrimination on the grounds of race, religion, sexual orientation, gender identity, disability, caste, culture, or age. The type and prevalence of violence and discrimination that women experience are often determined by how their gender interacts with these and other factors.

In the case of women's human rights, the principle of universality continues to be challenged. Some justify violations of women's human rights by placing precedence on cultural values and traditions, but this view ignores the fact that some practices and beliefs attributed to "culture" or "tradition" often shape women's lives in a way that subordinates and discriminates against them.

In fact, violence against women is rooted in a global culture that discriminates against women and denies them equal rights. Women today earn less than men, own less property than men, and have less access to education, employment, housing and health care. This global culture of discrimination denies women their human rights and legitimizes the violent appropriation of women's bodies for individual gratification or political ends. By limiting the universality of the human rights of women, cultural values rooted in unequal power relations between women and men become justification for the systematic denial of civil, cultural, economic, political and social rights.

States' responsibilities in relation to women's human rights

Each of the human rights treaties, and the human rights framework as a whole, are essential for the realization of women's full spectrum of rights. Whether abuses against women are committed by state or non-state actors, in the public or private spheres, the state is obliged to act. State obligations under international human rights law can be summarized under three categories:

Respect: The state has an obligation to respect women's human rights through its direct action, agents and structures of law. A state's constitution must recognize equality between women and men in all spheres; state or official actors must be held accountable when they perpetrate violence against women; private actors who perpetrate violence against women must be prosecuted.

Protect: The state has an obligation to protect women's human rights. The state must take all necessary measures to prevent individuals or groups from violating the rights of each individual. As such, the state must take affirmative steps to prevent direct and indirect discrimination against women. Women must be fairly represented in government and have legal access to all forms of employment.

Fulfill: The state is also required to fulfill the human rights of women by ensuring opportunities for individuals to obtain what they need and to provide that which cannot be secured by personal efforts. This obligation ranges from providing a healthy environment, clean water, food, housing and education, to creating the conditions necessary for women's organizations to form and function.

International law has developed the standard of due diligence as a way to measure whether a state has acted with sufficient effort to live up to its responsibilities to respect, protect and fulfill human rights. This standard has been explicitly incorporated into United Nations standards, such as the DEVAW, which says that states should "exercise due diligence to prevent, investigate and, in accordance with national legislation, punish acts of violence against women, whether those acts are perpetrated by the state or by private persons." Increasingly, U.N. mechanisms monitoring the implementation of human rights treaties, the U.N. independent experts, and courts at the national and regional level are using this concept of due diligence as their measure for assessing the compliance of states with their obligations to protect bodily integrity. Any act of violence against women perpetrated in the public or private sphere whether by state or non-state actors invokes the due diligence obligations of States to prevent, investigate, punish and provide compensation for all acts of violence.

Violence against women will continue until those responsible are held accountable under domestic laws in accordance with international human rights and humanitarian law. Factors contributing to impunity for crimes of violence against women are many, and include:

- An overall climate of indifference towards many forms of violence;
- Tacit acceptance of rape and other sexual violence as unavoidable;
- Threats and reprisals against those who reveal abuses;
- Laws granting amnesty to perpetrators as part of peacemaking "deals".

Governments have a responsibility to ensure that violence against women is punished in accordance with international standards for fair trials, and to that end, that the judicial system in their country functions independently of the government, and that law enforcement, judicial officials, and security forces receive adequate training to prevent violence and assist survivors. Despite such obligations, many countries have discriminatory laws that make it difficult for women to access justice, or their laws are interpreted in such a way as to facilitate impunity.

For example, when violence against women is committed in the context of armed conflict, national courts may lack jurisdiction over soldiers who are foreign nationals or it may be impossible to seek their extradition. The code of military law may not expressly address violence against women.

What should the United States government do?

Amnesty International U.S. urges the United States government to take four policy steps to help end violence against women globally. The United States should:
Pass the International Violence Against Women Act, which will:

- Make ending violence against women and girls a top diplomatic and foreign assistance priority for the United States by supporting and improving coordination of existing U.S. anti-gender-based violence efforts across the whole of government.
- Support survivors, hold perpetrators accountable, and prevent gender-based violence.
- Address violence against women and girls comprehensively and multi-sectorally by supporting health, legal, economic, education and humanitarian assistance sectors and incorporating violence prevention and response into such programs;
- Codify and implement the U.S Strategy to Prevent and Respond to Gender-Based Violence Globally, the first government-wide effort of its kind to address violence against women and girls globally across sectors, in five select countries which have a high incidence of violence against women;
- Permanently authorize the Office of Global Women's Issues in the State Department, as well as the position of the Ambassador-at-Large for Global Women's Issues, who is responsible for coordinating activities, policies, programs, and funding relating to gender integration and women's empowerment internationally, including those intended to prevent and respond to violence against women;
- Alleviate poverty and increase the cost effectiveness of foreign assistance by investing in women;
- Prevent violence by transforming social norms about the acceptability of it by engaging men and boys and supporting public awareness programs to change attitudes that condone, and at times encourage, violence against women and girls, as well as men and boys, and will emphasize community-based solutions;
- Enable the U.S. government to develop a faster and more efficient response to violence against women in humanitarian emergencies and conflict-related situations; and,
- Build the effectiveness of overseas non-governmental organizations — particularly women's non-governmental organizations—in addressing violence against women.

The IVAWA provides a comprehensive approach to address these priorities within a human rights framework by enhancing the efficacy and efficiency of existing U.S. government programs that tackle gender-based violence.

Pass the Women, Peace and Security Act which will:

- Increase women's meaningful inclusion in peace-building and conflict prevention processes;
- Protect women and girls from gender-based violence in conflict and post-conflict settings;
- Ensure women and girls have equitable access to humanitarian assistance;

- Require the State Department and U.SID to report to Congress on progress under the U.S. National Action Plan on Women, Peace and Security to promote women's participation in peace building and conflict prevention processes;
- Ensure that each relevant U.S. government agency integrates women as equal partners into all efforts to prevent and mediate conflict, respond to humanitarian crises, promote and build peace and democracy, and rebuild post conflict;
- Incorporate comprehensive training programs on women's participation in peace and security matters for diplomatic, defense, and development personnel; and,
- Require robust monitoring and evaluation of the impact of U.S. foreign assistance on women's meaningful inclusion and participation and revise approaches to employ best practices.

The Women, Peace and Security Act recognizes the untapped potential and significant value that women bring to the peacemaking table. Half of all peace agreements around the world fail within the first five years. One missing component to creating a lasting and sustainable peace is the inclusion of those who are disproportionately and uniquely affected by conflict: women. The Act requires the U.S. to promote the meaningful inclusion and participation of women in all peace processes that seek to prevent, alleviate or resolve armed conflict, which will increase the likelihood of successful conflict resolution.

Promote reform of discriminatory law and policies

The United States has a responsibility to press for legislative reform and to facilitate implementation of laws and policies that ensure women the same rights as men. This is especially the case in areas of property rights, access to employment, access to health services, and education for women and girls, as well as on laws relating to citizenship, the rights to enter into marriage willingly, and to have the same legal rights as men as parents of their children.

The United States should provide assistance for legal reforms that promote and protect fulfillment of human rights for women and children, and facilitate contact and collaboration with international organizations, including the United Nations mechanisms, which can assist and advise legislatures on legal reforms and policy implementation to support women and children. The U.S. should also increase its training of foreign security forces on addressing violence against women in armed conflict and on military codes of conduct regarding sexual exploitation and abuse.

Ratify the Convention on the Elimination of All Forms of Discrimination Against Women

CEDAW is a landmark international agreement that affirms fundamental human rights and equality for women around the world. It offers countries a practical blueprint to achieve progress for women and girls by calling on each ratifying country to overcome barriers to discrimination.

Around the world, CEDAW has been used to reduce sex trafficking and domestic abuse; provide access to education and vocational training; guarantee the right to vote; ensure the ability to work and own a business without discrimination; improve maternal health care; end forced marriage and child marriage; and ensure inheritance rights.

CEDAW and its Optional Protocol remain the only international treaties devoted to the rights of women. Partly due to the success of CEDAW, there have been significant advances in women's rights in the more than thirty years since CEDAW was adopted, although much remains to be done. The treaty has been ratified or acceded to by 187 countries, making it second only to the Convention on the Rights of the Child in terms of universal acceptance.

Adopted by the U.N. General Assembly in 1979, CEDAW obliges states parties to undertake legislative, administrative and practical measures to eliminate discrimination against women, in order to enable women to enjoy civil and political, as well as economic, social and cultural rights, as enshrined in the treaty. States parties are required to condemn discrimination against women, devise policies for its elimination and take steps to ensure the full development and advancement of women.

States parties undertake to submit reports to the Committee on the Elimination of Discrimination against Women at least every four years. The review of a state party report provides an opportunity for national-level review of implementation and the identification of obstacles which impede the enjoyment of the rights protected by CEDAW. The outcome of these reviews, as contained in the concluding comments of the Committee on the Elimination of Discrimination against Women, provide an important benchmark for measuring present compliance and future progress for the state party, civil society and different U.N. actors seeking to integrate them into country-based initiatives.

CEDAW is a tool that women around the world are using effectively to bring about change in their conditions. CEDAW ratification has encouraged the development of citizenship rights in Botswana and Japan, inheritance rights in Tanzania, and property rights and political participation in Costa Rica. CEDAW has fostered development of domestic violence laws in Turkey, Nepal, South Africa, and South Korea and anti-trafficking laws in Ukraine and Moldova.

The ratification of human rights treaties is a basic but essential step which every government can take to demonstrate its commitment to protecting human rights. When a government becomes a party to international human rights treaties, it affirms to the international community its determination to respect the dignity and worth of the human person.

Acceptance of international obligations helps to establish more durable commitments in the field of human rights protection. Adherence to these instruments not only invigorates domestic efforts at implementation but also preserves the achievements of today's governments against retrogression by those of tomorrow. Adherence by all states to these important instruments would be a major step forward in the further development and strengthening of international human rights protection for the benefit of all people.

The United States has a legacy of promotion and defense of human rights. However, the United States is one of only seven countries that have not yet ratified CEDAW, including Iran, South Sudan, Somalia, Palau, and Tonga. As such, the United States has the dubious distinction of being the only country in the Western Hemisphere and the only industrialized democracy that has not ratified this treaty. The U.S. Government's failure to ratify serves as a disincentive for other governments to uphold CEDAW's mandate and their obligations under it to end discrimination against women.

Ratification of CEDAW would strengthen the United States as a global leader in standing up for women and girls and provide a path for the full realization of women's human rights globally. With U.S. ratification, CEDAW would become a much stronger instrument in support of women's struggles to achieve the full realization of their human rights. Amnesty International believes that ratification would be a critical demonstration of the U.S. government's commitment to women's equal protection and equality of treatment before the law.

Amnesty International strongly urges the Senate to use this hearing as a meaningful step in the ratification of CEDAW. In addition, we urge the Senate to not attach any limiting interpretations, declarations and reservations to the ratification of CEDAW and to ensure that all U.S. laws, policies and practices conform to the principles espoused in CEDAW.

The abduction of over almost 300 schoolgirls in Nigeria provides us with a poignant example of why these recommendations are necessary.

In April, Boko Haram kidnapped hundreds of girls from their school in the town of Chibok. Boko Haram is an Islamist armed group that has waged a brutal insurgency in northeast Nigeria, carrying out similar abductions on a smaller scale in the past. Nearly two months later, the majority of the girls remain in captivity, and it is feared that the girls may face sexual violence or trafficking.

A life free from violence is a fundamental human right. Yet nearly a billion women around the world will not have that freedom.

To affect real change in the lives of women globally, action is needed now, and the United States must continue to be a leader on this issue by ratifying CEDAW and by passing legislation such as the International Violence Against Women Act and the Women, Peace and Security Act.

Chair Boxer, Senator Paul, and members of the Committee, on behalf of the abducted Nigerian schoolgirls and the nearly one billion women around the world who have experienced gender-based violence, Amnesty International U.S thanks you for holding this important hearing and urges you to take swift action.

Thank you.

––––––––––

STATEMENT SUBMITTED FOR THE RECORD
BY SECOND CHANCE EMPLOYMENT SERVICES

We, Second Chance Employment Services, wish to thank Chair Barbara Boxer and Ranking Member Rand Paul of the Senate Foreign Relations Subcommittee on International Operations and Organizations, Human Rights, Democracy, and Global Women's Issues for convening this hearing on "Combating Violence and Discrimination Against Women: A Global Call to Action." We call on the Senate Foreign Relations Committee and the U.S. Senate to move forward to pass the International Violence Against Women Act (IVAWA) and to ratify CEDAW in this Congress. These tools will give the United States greater clout to urge other countries to take all necessary steps to combat discrimination and violence against women and girls.

Gender-based violence (GBV) is the most widespread human rights violation in every part of the world. The well-documented cases of using rape as a weapon of war in the Congo, acid attacks on the faces of girls going to school in Afghanistan, the 2012 shooting of Pakistani education and women's rights activist, Malala Yousafzai, by the Taliban, and the recent horrific sexual assaults and hanging of girls and young women in India are only the most visible evidence of pervasive violence against women and girls. Unfortunately, intimate partner violence, often less visible, is also an epidemic, affecting 35 percent of women globally every year. Women have organized campaigns calling on their governments not only to adopt laws to provide services and safety for women and their children, bring perpetrators of violence to justice, educate the public, and engage boys and men, but also to address the underlying causes of discrimination and gender inequalities.

In addressing violence against women, many countries have been aided by the Convention on the Elimination of All Forms of Discrimination Against Women (CEDAW), also known as the women's equality treaty. CEDAW considers gender-based violence—that is, violence directed at women and girls just because they are female—to be a form of discrimination under the Convention, because such violence impairs or nullifies women's full enjoyment of their basic human rights.

CEDAW offers countries a practical blueprint to achieve progress for women and girls by calling on each ratifying country to overcome barriers to discrimination. For example, when activists in Afghanistan proposed the Law on the Elimination of Violence Against Women, they looked to CEDAW as a model to guide their approach. The South Korean Women's Movements Against Gender Violence looked to CEDAW to propose laws on domestic violence, which were then adopted by the government. Mexico, in adopting its General Law on Women's Access to a Life Free from Violence, drew on CEDAW, among other international and regional treaties. Following recommendations from the CEDAW Committee,

Mexico is now training its federal judiciary in human rights, gender-based violence and non-discrimination along with CEDAW to promote women's access to justice. In line with recommendations of the CEDAW Committee, Turkey enacted the Protection of the Family and Prevention of Violence against Women Law in 2012. Other examples of how CEDAW has been used to combat violence against women can be found in Recognizing Rights, Promoting Progress: The Global Impact of the Convention on the Elimination of all forms of Discrimination Against Women (www.icrw.org).

One hundred eighty-seven countries have ratified CEDAW. The United States is one of only seven countries in the world that has not ratified CEDAW, along with Iran, Somalia, Sudan, South Sudan, Palau, and Tonga. The United States' failure to ratify CEDAW undermines its leadership in the global fight to combat discrimination and violence against women, calls into question its credibility, and gives the appearance that the United States does not believe that reducing discrimination and violence against women should be a priority for governments around the world.

The scourge of violence against women and girls, however, threatens the basic security of the United States and the world. This epidemic not only affects women, their families and communities, but it also undermines the stability and prosperity of whole societies. This, in turn, has a direct impact upon U.S. foreign policy, security interests, and democracy and peace-building efforts. Gender-based violence against women does not stop at U.S. borders. Instead, it affects the well-being of U.S. citizens by contributing to global instability. The United States Senate must ratify CEDAW to enhance U.S. leadership in this area and support the important work to combat discrimination and violence against women being done by the U.S. Department of State and other Departments and agencies. CEDAW gives the United States another tool to advance the status of women and increase opportunity for prosperity for everyone.

Another mechanism central to the global prevention of and response to gender-based violence is the bipartisan International Violence Against Women Act, H.R. 3571/S. 2307, (IVAWA). IVAWA makes ending violence against women and girls a top diplomatic and foreign assistance priority by codifying, implementing, and giving congressional oversight to the ongoing U.S. Strategy to Prevent and Respond to Gender-Based Violence Globally (the Strategy). The Strategy, created by Executive Order in August 2012, calls for a coordinated, multi-sectoral response to gender-based violence—a process led by an Interagency Working Group to ensure maximum efficiency. IVAWA also permanently authorizes the State Department's Office of Global Women's Issues with the position of Ambassador-at-Large, who coordinates policies, programs, and funding relating to gender integration and women's empowerment internationally, including those intended to prevent and respond to gender-based violence (GBV). In addition, IVAWA authorizes the position of U.SID Senior Gender Coordinator, who is responsible for working with senior leadership and mission staff to fully integrate gender equality and female empowerment into U.SID's policies, programs, and strategies. These entities exist within the current structures of both agencies and would not add a new level of bureaucracy; rather, their existence contributes to greater accountability of the gender-focused policies and programming currently in place.

IVAWA would streamline and better coordinate anti-GBV programming across various U.S. government agencies, making addressing GBV a cornerstone of U.S. development and foreign policy. Since this legislation is aimed at coordinating and integrating existing programs, it does not require the appropriation of additional funding. The bill also focuses on preventing violence by transforming social norms about the acceptability of it. IVAWA recognizes that while women and girls disproportionately suffer from violence, men and boys experience targeted violence too. The bill intentionally utilizes the term GBV throughout, making it inclusive of all persons and not precluding programs from supporting men and boys. IVAWA will support public awareness programs to change attitudes that condone, and at times encourage, violence against women and girls, as well as men and boys, and will emphasize community-based solutions.

This integral piece of legislation would also increase legal and judicial protection to address gender-based violence; integrate programs to address gender-based violence into already existing health programs focused on child survival, health, and HIV/AIDS prevention, care, and treatment; reduce women and girls' vulnerability to violence by improving their economic status and educational opportunities; and, promote women's inclusion in civil and political life.

We believe the U.S. can and should be a leader in ending one of the biggest obstacles not only to U.S. national security but also global stability, development, prosperity, and human rights for all. Ending violence against women and girls, men and boys, and advancing women's equality is fundamental to the United States' national security interests and today is a cornerstone of America's foreign policy. Countries are more peaceful and prosperous when women have full and equal rights and opportunities. We acknowledge the leadership taken by the United States to condemn gender-based violence wherever it occurs—from Afghanistan and Guatemala, to Nigeria and the DRC, to the gender-based violence women experience every day in the United States—and we applaud the adoption of the Violence Against Women Act of 2013.

But today is a call to action because more needs to be done to combat gender-based violence globally. There are two more tools in the United States' toolbox that are before this Committee right now.

We, Second Chance Employment Services, call on the Senate Foreign Relations Committee and the U.S. Senate to move forward to pass the International Violence Against Women Act (IVAWA) and to ratify CEDAW in this Congress. These important tools will give the United States greater ability to work with and support other countries to take all necessary measures to prevent and one day end discrimination and violence against women and girls. The time to act is now.

STATEMENT SUBMITTED FOR THE RECORD BY INTERNATIONAL MEDICAL CORPS

Chairwoman Boxer, Ranking Member Paul, and members of the Subcommittee, on behalf of International Medical Corps, we thank you for holding this important and timely hearing.

International Medical Corps is a global, humanitarian, nonprofit organization dedicated to saving lives and relieving suffering through health care training and relief and development programs. Its mission is to improve the quality of life through health interventions and related activities that build local capacity in underserved communities worldwide. By offering training and health care to local populations and medical assistance to people at highest risk, and with the flexibility to respond rapidly to emergency situations,

International Medical Corps rehabilitates devastated health care systems and helps bring them back to self reliance.

Throughout the world, gender-based violence (GBV) is a pervasive public health and human rights issue that significantly affects women and girls. Worldwide, one in three women has been beaten, coerced into sex, or abused in some way, according to the United Nations. The toll is enormous, costing billions of dollars in social, judicial, and health costs, in addition to lost wages and productivity, and incalculable physical and emotional hardship.

Despite the seriousness of this issue, services to prevent and appropriately respond to GBV are still inadequate. This is particularly true in emergency settings, where women and girls face increased risks of violence.

Since 2005, International Medical Corps has worked with communities and service providers to address violence against women and girls in diverse and challenging environments such as Afghanistan, Philippines, Syria, Central African Republic, Iraq, DRC and Russia. As risks and types of violence vary across cultures, countries and regions, International Medical Corps develops context-specific approaches to increase protection for women and girls and to respond to the needs of survivors of violence.

International Medical Corps' core programming activities are implemented at the community level, where close collaboration with local service providers and grassroots social support networks is a highest priority.

Working closely with these actors allows us to design programs that are culturally appropriate and well tailored to the particular needs of targeted populations.

We strongly support and urge swift passage of S. 2307, the International Violence Against Women Act of 2014 (IVAWA) and believe its enactment is of paramount importance for the U.S. government in prioritizing an end to violence against women and girls globally. This violence threatens peace and stability, hinders recovery and development, and is a barrier to women and girls fully enjoying and exercising their rights.

International Medical Corps commends these bipartisan efforts to continue this vital and urgent work to ending violence against women and girls' front and center of diplomatic efforts. S. 2307 would facilitate the allocation of key human resources, funding and space for coordination that this issue critically needs for strategic and lasting change to take place. We also welcome the legislation's recognition of the importance of assistance to both preventing violence against women and girls, as well as responding to the needs of survivors in their road to recovery.

Once again, International Medical Corps applauds you for your ongoing leadership and commitment in creating a forum to discuss and guide our efforts, as we join together to end gender-based violence around the world.

STATEMENT SUBMITTED FOR THE RECORD BY VARIOUS ORGANIZATIONS

We, the 74 undersigned organizations, wish to thank Chair Barbara Boxer and Ranking Member Rand Paul of the Senate Foreign Relations Subcommittee on International Operations and Organizations, Human Rights, Democracy, and Global Women's Issues for convening this hearing on ''Combating Violence and Discrimination Against Women: A Global Call to Action.'' We call on the Senate Foreign Relations Committee and the U.S. Senate to move forward to pass the International Violence Against Women Act (IVAWA) and to ratify the Convention on the Elimination of all forms of Discrimination Against Women (CEDAW) in this Congress. These tools will give the United States greater clout to urge other countries to take all necessary steps to combat discrimination and violence against women and girls.

Gender-based violence (GBV) is the most widespread human rights violation in every part of the world. The well-documented cases of using rape as a weapon of war in the Congo, acid attacks on the faces of girls going to school in Afghanistan, the 2012 shooting of Pakistani education and women's rights activist, Malala Yousafzai, by the Taliban, and the recent horrific sexual assaults and hanging of girls and young women in India are only the most visible evidence of pervasive violence against women and girls. Unfortunately, intimate partner violence, often less visible, is also an epidemic, affecting 35 percent of women globally every year. Women have organized campaigns calling on their governments not only to adopt laws to provide services and safety for women and their children, bring perpetrators of violence to justice, educate the public, and engage boys and men, but also to address the underlying causes of discrimination and gender inequalities.

In addressing violence against women, many countries have been aided by the Convention on the Elimination of All Forms of Discrimination Against Women (CEDAW), also known as the women's equality treaty. CEDAW considers gender-based violence—that is, violence directed at women and girls just because they are female—to be a form of discrimination under the Convention, because such violence impairs or nullifies women's full enjoyment of their basic human rights.

CEDAW offers countries a practical blueprint to achieve progress for women and girls by calling on each ratifying country to overcome barriers to discrimination. For example, when activists in Afghanistan proposed the Law on the Elimination of Violence Against Women, they looked to CEDAW as a model to guide their approach. The South Korean Women's Movements Against Gender Violence looked to CEDAW to propose laws on domestic violence, which were then adopted by the government. Mexico, in adopting its General Law on Women's Access to a Life Free from Violence, drew on CEDAW, among other international and regional treaties. Following recommendations from the CEDAW Committee, Mexico is now training its federal judiciary in human rights, gender-based violence and non-discrimination along with CEDAW to promote women's access to justice. In line with recommendations of the CEDAW Committee, Turkey enacted the Protection of the Family and Prevention of Violence against Women Law in 2012. Other examples of how CEDAW has been used to combat violence against women can be found in Recognizing Rights, Promoting Progress: The Global Impact of the Convention on the Elimination of all forms of Discrimination Against Women (www.icrw.org).

One hundred eighty seven countries have ratified CEDAW. The United States is one of only seven countries in the world that has not ratified CEDAW, along with Iran, Somalia, Sudan, South Sudan, Palau, and Tonga. The United States' failure to ratify CEDAW undermines its leadership in the global fight to combat discrimination and violence against women, calls into question its credibility, and gives the appearance that the United States does not believe that reducing discrimination and violence against women should be a priority for governments around the world.

The scourge of violence against women and girls, however, threatens the basic security of the United States and the world. This epidemic not only affects women, their families and communities, but it also undermines the stability and prosperity of whole societies. This, in turn, has a direct impact upon U.S. foreign policy, security interests, and democracy and peace building efforts. Gender-based violence against women does not stop at U.S. borders. Instead, it affects the well-being of all people in the United States by contributing to global instability. The Senate must ratify CEDAW to enhance U.S. leadership in this area and support the important work to combat discrimination and violence against women being done by the U.S. Department of State and other Departments and agencies. CEDAW gives the United States another tool to advance the status of women and increase opportunities for prosperity for everyone.

Another mechanism central to the global prevention of and response to gender-based violence is the bipartisan International Violence Against Women Act, H.R. 3571/S. 2307, (IVAWA). IVAWA makes ending violence against women and girls a top diplomatic and foreign assistance priority by codifying, implementing, and giving congressional oversight to the ongoing U.S. Strategy to Prevent and Respond to Gender-Based Violence Globally (the Strategy). The Strategy, created by Executive Order in August 2012, calls for a coordinated, multi-sectoral response to gender-based violence—a process led by an Interagency Working Group to ensure maximum efficiency. IVAWA also permanently authorizes the State Department's Office of Global Women's Issues with the position of Ambassador-at-Large, who coordinates policies, programs, and funding relating to gender integration and women's empowerment internationally, including those intended to prevent and respond to gender-based violence (GBV). In addition, IVAWA authorizes the position of U.SID Senior Gender Coordinator, who is responsible for working with senior leadership and mission staff to fully integrate gender equality and female empowerment into U.SID's policies, programs, and strategies. These entities exist within the current structures of both agencies and would not add a new level of bureaucracy; rather, their existence contributes to greater accountability of the gender-focused policies and programming currently in place.

IVAWA would streamline and better coordinate anti-GBV programming across various U.S. government agencies, making addressing GBV a cornerstone of U.S. development and foreign policy. Since this legislation is aimed at coordinating and integrating existing programs, it does not require the appropriation of additional funding. The bill also focuses on preventing violence by transforming social norms about the acceptability of it. IVAWA recognizes that while women and girls disproportionately suffer from violence, men and boys experience targeted violence too. The bill intentionally utilizes the term GBV throughout, making it inclusive of all persons and not precluding programs from supporting men and boys. IVAWA will support public awareness programs to change attitudes that condone, and at times encourage, violence against women and girls, as well as men and boys, and will emphasize community-based solutions.

This integral piece of legislation would also increase legal and judicial protection to address gender-based violence; integrate programs to address gender-based violence into already existing health programs focused on child survival, health, and HIV/AIDS prevention, care, and treatment; reduce women and girls' vulnerability to violence by improving their economic status and educational opportunities; and, promote women's inclusion in civil and political life.

We believe the United States can and should be a leader in ending one of the biggest obstacles not only to U.S. national security but also global stability, development, prosperity, and human rights for all. Ending violence against women and girls, men and boys, and advancing women's equality is fundamental to the United States' national security interests and today is a cornerstone of America's foreign policy. Countries are more peaceful and prosperous when women have full and equal rights and opportunities. We acknowledge the leadership taken by the United States to condemn gender-based violence wherever it occurs—from Afghanistan and Guatemala, to Nigeria and the DRC, to the gender-based violence women experience every day in the United States—and we applaud the adoption of the Violence Against Women Act of 2013.

But today is a call to action because more needs to be done to combat discrimination and gender-based violence globally. There are two more tools in the United States' toolbox that are before this Committee right now.

We, 74 undersigned organizations, call on the Senate Foreign Relations Committee and the U.S. Senate to move forward to pass the International Violence Against Women Act (IVAWA) and to ratify CEDAW in this Congress. These important tools will give the United States greater ability to work with and support other countries to take all necessary measures to prevent and one day end discrimination and violence against women and girls. The time to act is now.

9to5
American Association of University Women
American Civil Liberties Union
American Jewish Committee
American Jewish World Service
American Psychological Association
Amnesty International U.S
Anti-Defamation League
Baha'is of the United States
Better World Campaign California Women's Agenda
Center for Gender & Refugee Studies
The Center for Health and Gender Equity
Center for Reproductive Rights
Communications Workers of America
Decisions In Democracy International
Demos
Equality Now
Feminist Majority
Freedom House
Futures Without Violence
Gender Action
GlobalSolutions.org
Guatemala Human Rights Commission Hadassah, The Women's Zionist Organization of America, Inc.
Human Rights Advocates

Human Rights Watch
The Hunger Project
IMA World Health
Institute for Science and Human Values, Inc.
The Interfaith Center of New York
International Psychoanalytical Association
Jacob Blaustein Institute for the Advancement of Human Rights
Jewish Board of Family and Children's Services
Jewish Women International
Jewish World Watch
The Leadership Conference on Civil and Human Rights
MomsRising
The National Conference of Puerto Rican Women, Inc.
National Council of Jewish Women
National Council of Women's Organizations
National Education Association
National Network to End Domestic Violence
National Organization for Women
National Women's Law Center
Pathfinder International
Peaceful Families Project
Population Action International

The Roosevelt Institute, Women and Girls Rising Program
Tahirih Justice Center
UJA-Federation of New York
United Methodist Women
United Nations Association of the United States of America
U.S. National Committee for U.N. Women
U.S. Women and Cuba Collaboration
U.S. Women Connect
Vital Voices Global Partnership
Women Donors Network
Women Employed
Women Enabled
Women for Women International
Women Graduates-USA
Women Legislators' Lobby
WomenNC
Women Thrive Worldwide
Women Watch Afrika, Inc.
Women's Action for New Directions
Women's Business Development Center
Women's Campaign International
Women's City Club of New York
Women's Intercultural Network
Women's U.N. Report Network
YWCA U.S
Zonta International